www.blue-way.net

Ulrich Golüke, born in 1952 in Neuwied, Germany is a systems dynamicist by training and has worked for the last twenty-five years extensively with scenarios. With others, he built up and ran for a number of years the Scenario Unit of the World Business Council for Sustainable Development. As a freelancer he has worked worldwide with companies, universities, foundations and students. He designs and delivers workshops and projects, builds computer models, gives speeches and writes. He is a visiting professor at the Business School of Lausanne where he teaches a course on scenario planning. He has lived in Wales, the United States, Norway, France, Germany and Switzerland.

Generous Respect

The next story of humanity

Ulrich Golüke

Bibliografische Information der Deutschen Nationalbibliothek: Die Deutsche Nationalbibliothek verzeichnet
diese Publikation in der Deutschen Nationalbibliografie;
detaillierte bibliografische Daten sind im Internet über
http://dnb.dnb.de abrufbar.

Photocredits:

fotolia.com #158374838 © GooDAura
fotolia.com #192986946 © dbrus
fotolia.com #121769756 © freshidea
Shutterstock.com #139005923 © Mopic
fotolia.com #91804983 © freshidea
fotolia.com #116679022 © pzAxe
fotolia.com #90485745 © Rrraum

Herstellung und Verlag:
BoD – Books on Demand, Norderstedt

ISBN: 978-3752839685

www.blue-way.net

To E, who gave me Geborgenheit that lasted,
    almost a lifetime,

to J, who never gives up, despite the odds,

to V, whose love I squandered carelessly,
    so many lifetimes ago,

to B, who first pointed out to me, in a casual way,
    the existence of frames,

to L, who helped me make it through many a night,

to A, J & L, who asked for advice, and

to C, who urged me to "make it a really popular story"
    – I hope I did.

Contents

Generous Respect

The next story of humanity

PRELUDE

"It is clear that we have to change the way we arrange our socio-economic affairs, which will not be easy" says Moshe Vardi, professor of computer science at Rice University in Texas. He predicts that machines will destroy half of all the jobs over the coming 30 years. The industrial revolution started in the 18th century, and we needed roughly 200 years to build a modern social welfare state, which is, in a way, an answer to that revolution. The next 50 years will force us to reinvent society again, but in a much shorter time. The question is which institutional mechanisms or settings society will develop as an answer to the fourth industrial revolution, whose revolutionary character we are fully aware of."[1]

This book is the story about the ongoing shift in the way we all look at the world, and thus organize our world. All of us alive today grew up during the reign of the economic narrative, which tells the stories of our lives as a series of transactions, whose ideal is growth and whose behavior is to maximize profit. Its promise, which is very attractive when you are dirt poor, is ever-growing wealth. It shapes the way we see, act, dream and hope. It limits and confines <u>what we think</u> is possible. Lately, though, that frame

1   Translated by me from http://www.zeit.de/kultur/2016-12/automatisierung-arbeitsgesellschaft-roboter-utopie-kommunismus/seite-2   The original, in German, goes like this: "Moshe Vardi, Professor für Computerwissenschaften an der Rice University in Texas, hält von einem generellen Müßiggang wenig. Er sagt: „Ich bin sehr skeptisch gegenüber solch grenzenlosem Optimismus. Es ist aber klar, dass wir die Art, unsere sozio-ökonomischen Angelegenheiten zu arrangieren, ändern müssen, was nicht einfach sein wird." Vardi prognostiziert, dass Maschinen in den nächsten 30 Jahren die Hälfte aller Arbeitsplätze vernichten werden. „Die Industrielle Revolution begann im 18. Jahrhundert und wir brauchten rund 200 Jahre, um einen modernen sozialen Wohlfahrtsstaat aufzubauen, der ja eine Antwort auf die Industrielle Revolution ist. Die nächsten 50 Jahre werden uns zwingen, die Gesellschaft neu zu erfinden, aber in einer sehr viel kürzeren Zeit."

is showing signs of wear and tear. Ending in Tomáš Sedláček's indictment that "the only thing remaining for us is growth – growth which knows nothing but itself, because it has no goal to measure. The feeling of aimlessness binds it to meaninglessness and homelessness"[1]

Once old frames have lost their ability to help us find meaning in our everyday lives, a new one emerges. We are witnessing such an emergence of a new frame, built on relations, generosity and respect. This book is about the possibility to change our lives and our societies that both have become empty, wasted and mean. This book is about hope.

What follows is my contribution to the conversation about what kind of life we might want to live. Read, enjoy and criticize it - but above all use it as a trigger to ponder what kind of life *you* and your loved ones may want to live. And then live it.

Note about footnotes

Footnotes disrupt the flow of the text. Yet I use them for sources and explanations, because we live in a time of lies and networks that pretend to be social.

---

2   Tomáš Sedláček, 2013, Economics of Good and Evil: The Quest for Economic Meaning from Gilgamesh to Wall Street, Oxford University Press, pg. 241, ISBN 978-0199322183

BEFORE THE BEGINNING

If I were to ask you how you decide what you decide, you most likely will talk about facts, constraints and truths. About weighing the pros and cons, about listening to a friend, celebrity or influencer whom you admire and who's judgment you trust. You might mention the hidden persuaders[1]. Finally, you may talk about your intuition and your excellent gut feeling.

While true, all of that happens within a narrative frame - a story which comes long *before* any of the considerations above. The catch is that these frames are so much a part of us, that we don't recognize them as such. We may think we have 20/20 vision, but it is the frame we use, almost always subconsciously, that limits, shapes and distorts what we see, notice and pay attention to. The frame largely determines what we consider possible, how we shape our responses and deliver our re-actions. We really do only hear what we want to hear, and disregard the rest[2].

This is not a shortcoming of ours. On the contrary, it is a brilliant way to make it through the day, the seasons, in fact through life. As Shiller and Akerlof point out in their book *Animal Spirits*: "The human mind is built to think in terms of narratives, of sequences of events with an integral logic and dynamic that appear as a unified whole. ... Life could be 'just one damn thing after another' if it weren't for these stories."[3]

---

1   Vance Packard, 1957, *The Hidden Persuaders*, Random House Inc, New York, ISBN: 9780679500308
2   Unless you work in a ministry of propaganda, or an ad-agency
3   Shiller & Akerlof, 2009, *Animal Spirits: How Human Psychology Drives the Economy*, Princeton, ISBN 978-069114233-3, pg. 51

Yuval Harari takes this idea one step further: he elevates our human ability to create collective narratives about things that don't exist to what he calls the cognitive revolution; and to which he traces the fact that Homo sapiens dominates the earth[1].

These are not just the idle musings of some, admittedly very clever, people, there seems to be a neurological basis for what they write. Kahneman in his book *Thinking, Fast and Slow*[2] writes of countless psychological and neuro-psychological experiments that strongly suggest that we use two modes of orienting ourselves in the reality that surrounds us. He calls them 'system 1' (fast) and 'system 2' (slow). The first is the one we use most of the time and it organizes what we see, hear, read, smell, touch etc. very fast into a coherent narrative, if need be at the expense of factual truth. This system 1 is impulsive, emotional, automatic and above all, fast. Within the blink of the proverbial eye it judges danger and pleasure and gets you to react in an appropriate manner. Its mechanism of choice is to create in your mind internally coherent stories that 'explain' what is going on and what to do about it.

The other system, system 2, is conscious, deliberate, considerate and, well, slow. While we are able to use it to distinguish between truth and fiction, it requires an effort which we often do not make. Thus, we gladly use existing framing narratives that 'explain the world to us'.

---

1   Harari, YN, 2015, *Sapiens: A Brief History of Humankind*, Harper, ISBN 9780062316097. An excerpt from chapter 2 on his website is well worth reading: http://www.ynharari.com/power-and-imagination/articles/the-most-important-things-in-the-world-exist-only-in-our-imagination/ accessed March 2016

2   Daniel Kahneman, *Thinking, Fast and Slow*, Penguin, ISBN 978-0141033570

Given all the things we have to attend to using such frames 'ready-made off the shelves' is a smart move – until the frame is no longer a good enough representation of the real world. When that happens, it's time to work on a new one, better suited for the reality at hand.

These framing narratives are our windows onto the world. Just like real windows in their window-frames they can be tiny, vast, dirty, clean, distorting or completely invisible[1]. Even though we hardly ever think about them - unless we are professional window cleaners[2] - they totally determine what we see. And if they become collective, they determine the ways that societies, and all the members of that

---

1   We all have seen videos of people bumping into glass partitions they thought weren't there. Some of us have even done the bumping all ourselves.
2   Van Morrison, *Cleaning Windows,* © Universal Music Publishing Group

society, choose to see, act upon and interpret the world around them. That, in a way, is the bad news.

The good news is that these collective frames are not cast in stone. You can clean your windows - at

least once in a while; you can even replace them and make the opening larger! Similarly, collective societal frames can and have been changed in the past. Not in some haphazard or arbitrary way, mind you. Because narrative frames are purposeful. They have a task to do. What is their task?

The task of frames

Glad you asked: the task of narrative frames is to create meaning, direction and structure, and by doing so, help answer the question of what is a life worth living. As Shiller and Akerlof note, without them life's just one damn thing after another. To avoid that fate, we have become the story-telling animal: "Only nature knows neither memory nor history. But man – let me offer you a definition – is the story-telling animal. Wherever he goes he wants to leave behind not a chaotic wake, not an empty space, but the comforting marker-buoys and trail-signs of stories. He has to go on telling stories. He has to keep making them up. As long as there's a story, it's alright."[1] Echoes of Kahneman's 'system 1'.

All strong narrative frames are fractal[2]. They exist at the same time on many levels and are intricately linked: individual, family, group, society, humanity - yesterday, today, tomorrow, next week, next year, eternity. For the rest of this short book, I am focusing my attention on the level of humanity, in the somewhat longer term.

To let you catch your breath, to get you a little more into the spirit of frames, to give you a feeling for how they can be both the most liberating and at the same time the most constricting partner in your life, allow me to take you on a breezy detour through frames of the past[3].

Frames of the past

At the level of humanity, frames are longer lasting, typically hundreds of years, and since the dawn of time, there have been four. They are the heroic, the religious, the scientific and the economic frame. A good way to talk about them in a brisk way is to

1 Swift G, 1992, *Waterland*, Picador, London ISBN 9780330336321
2 A fractal is a never-ending pattern. Fractals are infinitely complex patterns that are self-similar across different scales. They are created by repeating a simple process over and over in an ongoing feedback loop. Driven by recursion, fractals are images of dynamic systems – the pictures of Chaos. Geometrically, they exist in between our familiar dimensions. Fractal patterns are extremely familiar, since nature is full of fractals. For instance: trees, rivers, coastlines, mountains, clouds, seashells, hurricanes, etc. http://fractalfoundation.org/resources/what-are-fractals/ accessed March 2016
3 If you prefer literary fiction, a great way to get into the spirit of frames is Jonas Karlsson, 2015, *The Room*, Hogarth, an imprint of Penguin Random House, ISBN 9780804139984

highlight each frame's promise, ideal, actors, language, behavior and energy[1]. If you arrange this in a table, it looks like this[2]:

	Hero	Religion	Science	Economy	
Promise					
Ideal					
Actors					
Language					
Behavior					
Energy					

If you are the pondering type, if you always pause a bit before you open the shutters on your windows, spend a little time on trying to fill in the blanks. This is *not* a test to see if you get it right - there really is no right or wrong - it is more an exercise to give you a feeling for frames. They are real, and not frightening at all, once you spend a little time with them and inside them. They don't bite, and I promise I won't leave you alone with them - I'll take you by the hand as I walk you through them.

---

1 This review of the four frames and the structure to talk about them come from Betty Sue Flowers during many years of working on projects together and numerous conversations. A free written account is Betty S Flowers, 2007, *The American dream and the economic myth*, Fetzer Institute, Kalamazoo, Mich., Series: Essays on deepening the American dream, essay no. 12. available here: http://www.fetzer.org/resources/american-dream-and-economic-myth-deepening-american-dream-series and listed in the World Catalogue here: https://www.worldcat.org/title/american-dream-and-the-economic-myth/oclc/183705278&referer=brief_results

2 You can download all graphs and matrices in a larger size from www.blueway.net/GenerousRespectTheGraphs.pdf

Each narrative frame starts with a promise. The promise is the – promised[1] – outcome if you adhere, if you live by, if you accept the rules of the frame. Second, it has an ideal, which is "a conception of something in its perfection", as the dictionary informs us. Put more plainly, the ideal is the goal that a particular frame pushes, or nudges its members to strive towards. Doesn't mean it is ever reached, but it is always held up as the shining example. And worth making sacrifices for.

The other four criteria are archetypes. An archetype is a model after which other similar things are patterned, a prototype, the quintessence of something. Archetypes are not all-encompassing, for example, if the archetypical behavior of a dog is to be submissive, it does not mean that the dog is never bored, ill-behaved, aggressive or antagonistic. It just means that the quintessence of a dog is that he or she submits to someone else's authority.

Thus, each narrative frame has archetypical actors who carry, or who embody the narrative. The archetypical surf bum, for example, is young, male, long-haired, wears a neoprene suit (but not on Hawaii – and never neoprene boots!), smiles and is dangerously handsome - you get the picture. Again, it does not mean there are no female surf bums, also dangerously handsome, it just means the archetype is male and barefoot.

Each frame also has an archetypical language (think of legalese, or doctor talk, as archetypical examples in our world) in which it expresses itself and which its actors prefer to use. Furthermore, each frame

---

1   Not always realized

prescribes an archetypical way to behave. And it draws its energy from an archetypical source.

Enough gibberish, I'll walk, actually rush, you through the frames now one by one.

Hero

	Hero	Religion	Science	Economy	
Promise	Survival				
Ideal	Excellence				
Actors	Heroes Adversaries				
Language	Stories				
Behavior	Competition				
Energy	Solar				

The first and oldest frame is the heroic one. Even though it is the one whose heyday has long passed, we tend to know it very well. The hero's story is still a favorite way to tell any story, and if you read a Harry Potter book, or watch an episode of Game of Thrones, you know exactly what I mean. The promise of this frame is survival. Remember, the promise is not always realized, but what gave this frame its appeal at the time it ruled the world was that if you lived by its rules, you at least improved your chances of survival. The ideal of this narrative frame is excellence. The actors are heroes and their adversaries, and the language of the frame is stories. The archetypical behavior is competition, and the energy that fuels it is solar.

All founding myths of civilizations, Greek and most other plays, Steven Spielberg movies, even many sports events are staged as heroic clashes. Star Trek is a heroic story - with the one exception that the energy is not solar. Most children's stories, the ones we read when we put our children to bed, are examples of the heroic frame. This frame is so deeply ingrained in us that most of us can accurately recount what the hero's journey consists of. Can you? The answer is at the bottom of the page[1].

Even though it seems to be everywhere, the heroic frame is no longer the one humanity uses to create meaning for, nor to give direction to and put structure into our daily lives. Even children learn very quickly that these kinds of stories are make-believe. And despite all their magnificence and splendor, role-playing conventions are, well, about role-playing.

A word about the triangle at the bottom of the heroic column. This signals that each narrative frame capable of providing meaning, direction and structure to everyday life, to guide and to nudge members of the society towards leading lives worth living, needs to create conventions for conversations between Nature, Humans and the Spiritual. In the heroic frame Humans are at the apex of this triangle, they mostly converse with the Spiritual and take Nature as given - helpful or not, but given.

Religion

The second oldest frame is the religious narrative. Its promise is the good life, if not here on earth, then at least after your death. Its ideal is goodness,

---

1   The call, the preparation, trials and tribulations, the supreme ordeal, the homecoming.

the archetypical actors of this frame are saints and prophets, who reveal to us mere mortals profound insights - including what goodness actually is - that should guide our ways. The language is that of scriptures and prayers, the codifications of insights granted to the saints and prophets. Once codified, they are repeated over and over again. The expected behavior of this frame is obedience, to the letter of the codified scriptures and their interpreters. The energy, as before, is solar. The fundamental conversation of this frame has the Spiritual at its apex and is mostly between it and Humans. Nature if off to the side.

	Hero	Religion	Science	Economy	
Promise	Survival	A good life after death			
Ideal	Excellence	Goodness			
Actors	Heroes Adversaries	Saints Prophets			
Language	Stories	Scriptures Prayers			
Behavior	Competition	Obedience			
Energy	Solar	Solar			

Note that the *religious frame* is not the same as organized religions. Organized religions often have deep heroic strands in their DNA. Just witness the mercilessness with which many of them confront non-believers. That is competition, pure and simple and, far too often, to the death.

Science

Science is the third major narrative frame humanity used to create meaning, give direction and form structure out of the seemingly arbitrariness of human existence. The conversation triangle underwent a major shift. The Spiritual got sidelined, Nature took its place at the apex and Humans served Nature. "God is dead", declared Nietzsche in 1882[1].

	Hero	Religion	Science	Economy	
Promise	Survival	A good life after death	A good life here on earth		
Ideal	Excellence	Goodness	Truth		
Actors	Heroes Adversaries	Saints Prophets	Philosophers Scientists		
Language	Stories	Scriptures Prayers	Logic Mathematics		
Behavior	Competition	Obedience	Reason		
Energy	Solar	Solar	Solar		

This frame emerged during what we, with hindsight, call the period of Enlightenment. Humanity believed that understanding the Laws of Nature would give meaning, imply direction and form structure for the lives of everyday people so that they deeply and honestly felt they were living lives worth living.

The promise was that by understanding and harnessing the laws of nature, a good life was possible here on earth. If not for everybody, then at least for a few privileged – the rest could always hope for their rewards in the afterlife. The ideal of this frame became truth, its actors were scientists and philos-

1   Nietzsche, 1974, *The Gay Science*, Vintage, New York, ISBN 9780394719856

ophers who used the language of logic and mathematics. The behavior that shaped this frame was reason - and the energy still solar.

The images that emerge in front of your eyes are probably that of Galileo, of Michelangelo, of Hume and Copernicus. The men and women of science are often talked about in heroic terms, but that is due to the fact that we like our stories to be told this way - it catches attention, sells copies and gets clicks. But what they actually did was to lift the veil of mysticism and replace it with clarity of thought, logical inferences and deductive reasoning. They created and carried that frame. An honest scientist's ideal to this day is the truth, wherever it may lead him or her. Not surprisingly, the strongest sanctions of the scientific community is reserved for those who cheat.

Economy

	Hero	Religion	Science	Economy	
Promise	Survival	A good life after death	A good life here on earth	Matterial wealth for all, now	
Ideal	Excellence	Goodness	Truth	Growth	
Actors	Heroes Adversaries	Saints Prophets	Philosophers Scientists	Consumers Business	
Language	Stories	Scriptures Prayers	Logic Mathematics	Numbers Images	
Behavior	Competition	Obedience	Reason	Maximizing Advantage	
Energy	Solar	Solar	Solar	Fossil	

The fourth frame, the fourth window onto the world humanity has created, is the economic one. This is, in fact, the one all of us are living in. Which makes it so damn hard to recognize it as merely a frame. To most of us, it is the truth. Not in a scientific way, but in the way the cookie crumbles - THAT'S IT!

Since I want to convince you that frames are *variables*, I will spend the entire next chapter "The World as it is" to go into the detail of the economic story. Here, I will just give you a very high level overview, in the breezy style I used for the other frames.

The promise of this frame is material wealth for all, now. The ideal of the economic frame is growth, growth as we are learning, at almost any cost. The key actors are consumers and producers, engaging in endless transactions – the more the better. And as we transact, the economic story atomizes and destroys the web of relationships that make us humans human[1]. Note that it is not human beings that are acting, but only humans in as much as they consume or produce - economic man and woman. The language of this economic frame is images and numbers, which allow it to be the first truly global story – your mother tongue does not really prevent you from fully participating in this story, because you communicate with others through images, numbers and icons. The behavior of this story is that of maximizing advantage, very often in a relentless, one could even say, merciless, way. And, finally, this is the first story that is not driven by solar energy, but by the use of fossil fuels. An important point I will get back to in the next chapter.

---

1 And its servant, digitalization, accelerates and intensifies the smashing of relations – this is the 'business model' of the digital world, to be better able to manipulate you.

THE WORLD AS IT CURRENTLY IS: THE ECONOMIC STORY

By at two and sell at three
Anonymous

It is difficult to get people to take the idea of frames serious. The first three, the heroic, religious and scientific one, are all rejected, because for most of us they are so far away in time and experience that they are unfamiliar, and they don't resonate with us anymore. And for those who *do* live in them, the suggestion that they are frames, and changeable at that, is even more disturbing. It is the(ir) truth, after all.

Before we make fun of those who are elevating another frame to an ultimate truth, let us be humble and recognize that the economic story is for most of *us* the objective and unalterable truth. It is all we've ever known, it is in our bones. It is the mother milk we were fed when we formed our views of the world. So, let me start with the (heroic?) task of trying to convince you that the economic frame is but a frame, and, furthermore, one whose time has passed.

The promise is material wealth for all, now

As we drown in waste, choke on plastic debris, have an ecological footprint that translates into 1.5 planets – three if you are a European or North American reader – and have experienced rising inequality for at least the last three decades[1], it seems odd that the promise of this frame is material wealth. It seems less odd, even understandable, when you think back to the beginning of the dominance of the

---

1   World Inequality Report 2018, online at https://wir2018.wid.world/

economic frame, some 200 years ago. At that time, life was short, nasty and brutish. Life expectancy for the vast majority of us was around 30 years[1], and a bit longer in Europe. Poverty was the norm[2]. We lived at the very bottom of Maslow's hierarchy of needs[3]. At the bottom, where we all were at the start of the economic story, physiological needs dominate life: the struggle for food, shelter and security. All of which can be better met with (more) material supplies. As those were insufficient at the time we can rightly say that we lived in a material-constrained world. Thus, the promise of removing those constraints was a very powerful one. And it wasn't just a promise. Since we learned to harness fossil fuels, we could start on our long road of material growth, life got better for more and more of us and we gladly elevated growth to the ideal of the frame.

The ideal is growth

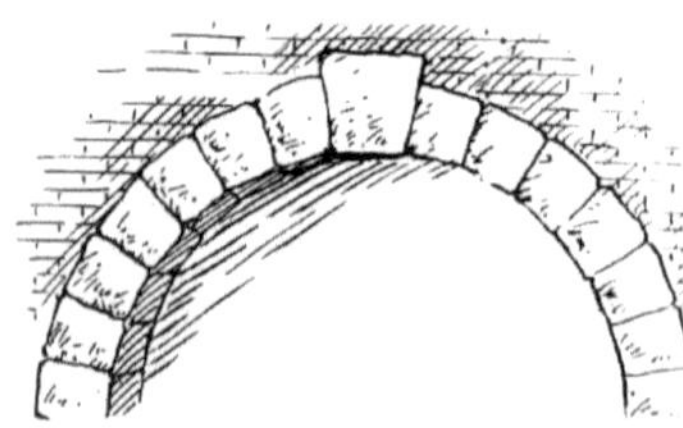

The ideal of a frame is the keystone of the whole edifice. It is the one that holds everything in place. The keystone of the economic story, its shining ideal, is growth. Even though growth is a double-edged sword: when you are little, say a fetus in your mother's womb, growth is not just wonderful, it is absolutely essential for you. But if you are an old person, and even if only a few of your cells are growing like

---

1   https://ourworldindata.org/life-expectancy
2   https://ourworldindata.org/grapher/world-population-in-extreme-poverty-absolute
3   Maslow, A.H. (1943). „A theory of human motivation". Psychological Review. 50 (4): 370–96. doi:10.1037/h0054346 You need to purchase a copy for around 12 USD

they did when you were a fetus, this is bad news, because it is code for cancer. Biology and life has a way to talk about "bad growth", they call it "cancerous growth". The economic frame does not. Here growth = good, no matter what. In fact, the frame goes so far as to call a decline 'negative growth'. It's like calling being kicked when you are down, 'negative admiration'. Sounds weird, doesn't it - but the economic frame thinks nothing of it.

If growth as an ideal is so odd, why did it get established in the first place? Because the economic frame as a giver of meaning, provider of direction and source of structure for the lives of everyday people emerged against a background of flatness. At the turn of the 19th century, say from 1750 to 1850, when the economic frame emerged, humankind could look back on thousands of years of no growth at all, in number of people, in life expectancy, in material wealth. The simple graph below has always impressed me[1]:

It shows the number of people on this earth over the last 2000 years. The horizontal axis is the years, so we are currently at the far-right end in the year 2018, and the ver-

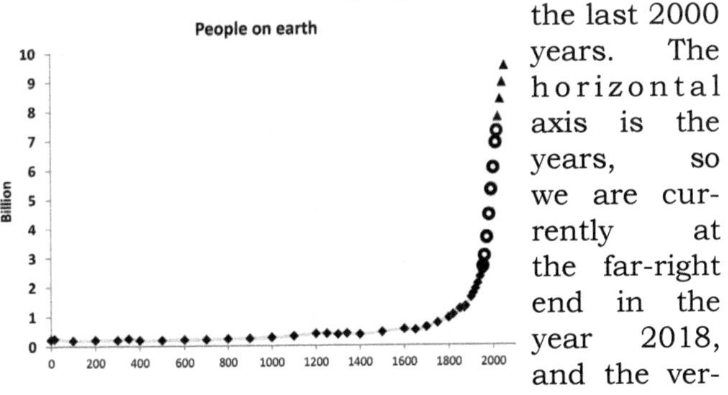

___

1   If you prefer moving pictures, take a look at gapminder.org http://www.gapminder.org/answers/how-did-the-world-population-change/   last accessed April 29, 2016

tical axis is number of people in billion[1]. As you can see, nothing much in terms of people on earth really happened from the year zero to 1800. A few hundred million of us tried to make a living and, on a good day, even make sense of our lives. Then in about the year 1800 things started to change: within 150 years or so, humanity grew from a few hundred million to about 2.5 billion. The last black diamond represents just about the year 1950 when something even more dramatic began to happen.

It also happens to be around the year of my birth, so the circles on the graph is the increase in the number of people on earth during my lifetime. The last circle is just about now. From 2.5 billion to a bit over 7 billion, in one lifetime.

Learned and wise people have made projections, and these are the triangles rising to well above 9 billion people in the next 35 years. Statistically speaking, I will see the first and maybe a bit of the second triangle and that'll be the end of my life – hopefully, you reading this are much younger and will, statistically at least, experience all of the triangles and a few in addition.

So, what has this graph to do with the economic story?

Well, the very first narrative frame we humans invented, the heroic one, happened at a time of very few people on earth, it was probably way, really way over on the left of the graph, even before the year zero. When the second frame, the religious one, was our sense making story, we are time-wise in the years 400 to 800, maybe to 1200, in any case at a time when there were, at least from today's vantage

---

1   A 1 with nine 0s

point, still very few people on earth. Then we come to the next frame, the scientific story, the one that cherished scientific inquiry and truth. The one we now call the period of enlightenment. This was in the 1600s or 1700s. From the late 1700s onwards, we, that is the number of us on this earth, really took off. Put yourself back not in today's vantage point but into the mindset of a person living around 1800 – and you'll have to conclude that to this person, things just grew and grew and grew and grew.

The growth in number of people was matched by growth in material wealth – fulfilling the promise of the frame ever more obviously. The data are not as available as for people, hence not as impressive, but if you want to dig deeper into this, have a look at Braudel's work.[1]

If growth happens all around you, it is quite understandable that a narrative frame emerged that put growth at the center. At first, for well over a hundred years, it worked very well indeed. The benefits were tangible: more food, less death, more things - and don't judge this from the perspective of a 21st century person drowning in things, but from the perspective of your great-grandparents - more choices, more security, more happiness.

But the fatal mistake - for *its* preeminence, not ours – which the economic narrative is making is that it accepts no limit. In fact, those who point them out are met with the disdain, contempt and hatred of a heretic. From ridicule to banishment, the punishment is meted out swiftly and without mercy.

---

1   Braudel F, 1979, *Civilization and Capitalism, 15th–18th Centuries*, translated by Siân Reynolds, vol. 1: The Structures of Everyday Life ISBN 0-06-014845-4, vol. 2: The Wheels of Commerce ISBN 0-06-015091-2, vol. 3: The Perspective of the World ISBN 0-06-015317-2, U of California Press

The actors are consumers and producers

The economic frame reduces humans to consumers and producers[1]. What might make perfect sense to an economist - those of the dismal science - is actually appallingly demeaning. It gives acceptance to the idea that I don't need to care the least bit about you, *except* if you have something to sell that I want, or if you want to buy something from me that I have. All that matters between you and me are the transactions we, well, transact. *All* the rest is by the way. This view takes away your dreams, your hopes, your fears, your worries, your health, your friendships, your ambitions, your failings, your scars, your beauty, your daydreams, your emotions, your uniqueness, your comfort, your doubts, your empathy, your curiosity - just about everything that makes a human being human. It leaves behind an empty shell of a being we call economic man and woman. Rational to a fault, but devoid of humaneness[2]. The implications are devastating.

If you are ill and need to go to the doctor, you are seen, in this view, first and foremost as a revenue generator, not as an ill person who needs help and comfort. Beware if you end up in a hospital where the head surgeon has a contract that pays a bonus for each transplantation. Beware of getting old, as all old-age homes are run for profit - even the ones run by charities. Your life will become subject to optimal cost benefit analysis. Optimal for whom? Revenue maximizing does not stop with airlines selling (tiny) seats, it is alive and well when taking care

---

1   In the jargon of the economic frame one would say: „The economic frames focuses on the human potential as consumers and producers, and grants these key attributes prominent and near-exclusive attention."

2   A good book that goes much deeper on this is Katrine Marçal, 2015, *Who Cooked Adam Smith's Dinner: A Story about Women and Economics*, Portobello Books, London UK, ISBN 9781846275647

(?) of the old, handling refugees, incarcerating criminals, teaching youngsters, raising kids.

Even when falling in love, revenue maximizing plays an increasingly important role. It used to be, in the quaint old days, that love was outside the economic realm. Admittedly, it didn't always work out. So up steps the economic frame to the rescue in the form of countless internet dating agencies that promise, nay guarantee, instant happiness, eternal bliss and out of this world sex. In my home country, one such agency advertises with the tagline "on our platform someone falls in love every 11 minutes" – but, trust me, only after your payment has been processed.

Education has also fallen prey to the economic mandate of growth. "You get what you pay for", an old Maine saying, has taken on a very ominous meaning in our current narrative frame.

There are many more realms of life that I could mention that have fallen under the sway of economic man and woman, but let me conclude this part by saying a few words about internet advertising. The rise, and so far, dominance, of companies like Google, Facebook and Apple rests on the simple proposition that by using their sites or products, you reveal continuously enormous amounts of your personal information to them. This information is then sold to others, who in turn wish to sell something to you. A string of ever-more personalized transactions. In many ways, this is the most clear-cut example that you exist in the economic story solely and exclusively as a consumer, as someone whose only role in life is to part with your money. How to get into your wallet and extract as much as possible is the only motivation. Nothing else is interesting about you -

nothing. You've become a pawn in a game that others play: "what's in it for them?" Some of us have the opportunity to learn this the hard way, when our wallets became empty. You are not even dropped like a hot potato - which implies disdain, not a nice, but a human emotion - you simply don't exist anymore. Silently, entirely, finally.

The language is numbers and images

Communication takes place in this narrative frame through images and numbers. This allowed the economic story to be the first global one. Regardless of your mother tongue, and regardless of your station in life, you can fully participate in this story, as long as you have some money to part with. A millionaire from China finds herself in this story, just like a beggar in Sweden, a dish-washer in America, just like a doctor in the Senegal. They can all talk to each other. They understand each other. They can give tips to each other on how "to make it"[1].

While it is on one hand wonderful that we can all talk to each other, there are two down-sides to this.

1) The fact that really everybody can talk to each other suggests a universality to the story that precludes learning. Learning requires an outside, an exterior. Something that by its mere presence challenges the inside, the accepted truths in the interior. If that challenge is not there - and if something is universal, there is nothing but itself - how do you begin to raise a question? No doubts, no learning. Chances are that the universality of the economic story is actually the reason for its demise. The nar-

---

1   Witness the enormous and ever-increasing amount of get-rich literature, videos and websites. They promise effortless riches, but only after you have paid for their mass produced 'exclusive' secrets.

rative, though seemingly invincible, can't adapt, because anything that could possibly put it in question, does not exist.

It dawned on me how far this suffocating universality actually goes when I read an interview with Ms. Herrmann from the Tageszeitung "taz". An exceptionally clear thinker who can convince you of the inevitability of the end of capitalism, but even she is unable to imagine any alternative and despite predicting the end of capitalism, warns vehemently against the chaos that will result when it does end[1].

2) The second down-side of the universal language of the economic story is the slow, but steady reduction in transmitting nuanced information. Numbers, except for the irrational ones, have the great advantage of clarity, precision and exactness. At the same time, they have the great disadvantage of removing even the last bit of ambiguity, of any hint of a room to maneuver. But that vagueness of natural language is the glue of human relation, it is what holds us and communities, nations and humankind together. Makes it harder to learn a foreign language, but trust me, makes your relationship with your loved ones last considerably longer.

We have learned how to count, but we've forgotten what counts. Numbers separate.

Images, the other leg of communicating the economic story, are said to be worth a thousand words. May well be true, but they also tightly prescribe what the sender of the message wants you to see. The sender no longer gives you any room to come up with own interpretations, imaginations or thoughts.

---

1 in German: http://www.deutschlandfunk.de/wirtschaftspolitik-warum-der-kapitalismus-im-prinzip-nicht.1184.de.html?dram:article_id=313835

Images, in short, control and oppress. Stalin knew this long before photoshop, when he pioneered the erasure from public pictures of people fallen from his grace.

The behavior is maximizing advantage

Having read this far, it won't come as a big surprise to you that the archetypical[1] behavior of the economic narrative is maximizing advantage. Not competition, mind you, but maximizing advantage. What is the difference? In a competition you stop once your opponent has lost. But when you maximize your advantage, there is no end. It goes on forever. It is a race that is never over. Because no matter how big your advantage already is, it could always be bigger still.

This gives the behavior of the economic frame a ruthlessness that takes your breath away. How did Tomáš Sedláček's put it more cryptically? "The feeling of aimlessness binds it to meaninglessness and homelessness"[2] More colloquially, we could say that if you always try to maximize your advantage, you live your lives empty and tired, and in the end, it amounts to a wasted life. The story of Sisyphus[3] comes to mind.

---

1   By now it won't come as a surprise to you that the economic frame has already taken over the very concept of archetypes for its own ends. It redefines them as „A System for the Management of Meaning". From a slideshow published by J Manley, a group strategy director at DBB, a worldwide ad agency, in their Chicago office, see http://www.slideshare. net/johnmanley/brand-archetype-overview accessed April 16, 2016. See also http://thebigstory.nl/brand-archetypes-content-strategy/ accessed April 16, 2016 and http://aamplify-demand.squarespace.com/archetypes/ also accessed April 16, 2016

2   Tomáš Sedláček, 2013, Economics of Good and Evil: The Quest for Economic Meaning from Gilgamesh to Wall Street, Oxford University Press, pg. 241, ISBN 978-0199322183

3   https://www.greekmyths-greekmythology.com/the-myth-of-sisyphus/

The internet economy is the latest and cleanest example - only challenged by the self-optimization of our bodies - of where maximizing advantage leads to: the winner really does take all, again and again. And rather than see through this injustice, we play

their game, because we want to be a winner too. Even though the odds are far, far less than winning any lottery you can think of.

We made it our game as well, because we are faithful believers in the economic story. We are fully participating, and even if it dawns on us that the rich will, *in the economic frame*, always get richer and the poor will always become poorer, we don't know how to break out. We may well be the blessed ones, for we shall inherit the kingdom of heaven, but meanwhile the top 1% make their getaway with all the loot.

While Braudel[1] still insists, when he writes about the beginnings of the economic story, that "[c]apitalists were human", he already notes the tendency

1   Braudel F, 1979, *Civilization and Capitalism, 15th–18th Centuries*, translated by Siân Reynolds, vol. 2: The Wheels of Commerce ISBN 0-06-015091-2, pg 402, U of California Press

of the economic story to favor "competition with-out competitors" (pg. 412-421). It is Karl Polanyi, who points out 200 years later, in 1944 in his *Great Transformation*, that life has become a mere adjunct to the economy[1]. Still, it took us another seventy years, another lifetime[2], for this to become patently obvious, even to the most indifferent observer.

The energy is fossil

How could growth, and its enabling cousin – maximizing advantage – become such a powerful driver in all our lives, spreading its tentacles into ever more realms, and showing no signs of stopping? It was possible because the rise of the economic story coincided with our ability to harness fossil fuels. I use the word 'coincide', because I am not sure what caused what. What is the chicken and what is the egg? If pushed, I'd even venture a guess that our ability to unlock the energy in fossil fuels came first. It paved the way for unprecedented changes in the way we humans eked out a living. Only once growth from the extraordinary productivity gains made possible by fossil fuels occurred, did the need arise to create a sense-giving narrative frame centered on growth and maximizing advantage.

Unless we work for an energy company, we tend to take unlimited cheap energy for granted. It is so seemingly abundant that we waste it to our hearts' content. We actually need to make an intellectual effort to grasp that this state of affairs is only 200

---

1 Karl Polanyi, 2001 [1944], *The Great Transformation, The Political and Economic Origins of Our Time*, Beacon Press, Boston, USA, ISBN: 978-080705643-1
2 Well, this *is* the planet of slow learners.

years old[1]. A mere blip in the history of humans. For most of humanity's time on earth the societal in- and outflow of energy was closely balanced. The surplus was tiny and could vanish completely and without notice. Repeatedly, famines and the other three deadly horsemen decimated the population.

The basal metabolic rate of a human being is about 3 Giga-Joules per year. That's what you get if you sum up the 2000 calories you should eat per day over a whole year[2]. Work done for some time now at the Institute of Social Ecology[3] at the University of Klagenfurt shows that a hunting and gathering society generates about 11 Giga-Joules per person per year, about 4 times the basal rate. An agrarian society generates very roughly around 50 Giga-Joules per person per year, about 16 times the basal rate. And our industrial society generates about 150 Giga-Joules per person per year, about 50 times the basal rate.

Two questions: One, what do we do with the excess energy over and beyond the basal rate we need to survive? Two, how are these amounts generated? In energy constrained societies, which the hunting & gathering and the agrarian societies are, *the extra energy is used for population growth* and the societal arrangements needed to support that growth[4]. In a hunting & gathering society the 'surplus' of

1   Two books that will help make that effort enjoyable are Smil V, 1994, *Energy in World History*, Westview Press, Boulder CO, USA, ISBN 9780813319025 and Sieferle RP, 2001, *The Subterranean Forest: Energy Systems and the Industrial Revolution*. Translated from the German original by Michael P. Osman. Cambridge: The White Horse Press, Isle of Harris, UK, ISBN 978-1874267539,

2   1 calorie = 4184 Joules * 365 days / Giga(1e9)

3   http://www.uni-klu.ac.at/socec/eng/inhalt/1.htm accessed April 16, 2016

4   We did not spend all the surplus energy on procreation, we also built pyramids, temples and cathedrals, canals, railroads and airports - and we flew to the moon and back.

8 Giga-Joules per person per year gives a population growth rate of very roughly 0.05 % per year[1]. In other words, it takes on average 1400 years for the population to double.

In an agrarian society the 'surplus' of about 50 Giga-Joules per person per year gives a population growth rate of very roughly 0.11 % per year[2]. In other words, it takes on average 630 years for the population to double, while the population growth *rate* doubles from 0.05 % per year to 0.11 % per year.

In our fossil fuel driven society, we have about 150 Giga-Joules per person per year 'left over' to 'spend on population growth', and, boy, we did. From 1800 onward, our population growth rate grew exponentially to reach 1.9 % per year during the 1980s and the early 1990s. Since then, the rate 'slowed down' to about 1.3 % per year. The former, 1.9 % per year, is a doubling of the population every 40 years - less than the average lifetime of a single human being. And even the latter, 1.3 % per year, is a doubling of the population over roughly 50 years. What took our hunting & gathering cousins 1400 years and our agrarian great-grandparents 630 years, we do in the blink of an eye. Now *that* is growth!

The 'slowdown' in the rate of population growth suggests, of course, that we decide to have children or

---

1   Gignoux, Henn, Mountain, 2011, *Rapid, global demographic expansions after the origins of agriculture*, Proceedings of the National Academy of Sciences 108 (15) 6044-6049, doi:10.1073/pnas.0914274108
2   calculated from the population graph a few pages back

not with additional criteria in mind[1], rather than pure energy 'surplus' alone. We are not, in other words, an energy constrained society any-more.

When I tried to answer the second question, *where does all this energy come from*, I also learned a lot. In the hunting & gathering and the agrarian societies all the energy there is comes from the sun. Sieferle et al. detail in their book "Das Ende der Fläche"[2] how agrarian societies managed to extract the 50 Giga-Joules per person per year through elaborate agricultural practices.

In our fossil fuel society, one could argue that, still, all the energy comes from the sun, but most of it by drawing down the stored kind, the kind that it took hundreds of millions of years to create, namely the fossil reserves. We are gorging in a few hundred years what it took a few hundred million years to create. In one single year we are completely using up what it took a million years to make. It is as if you save every day a glass of wine, and then one day, say on the last day of the year, you drink it in one big, nay, *huge* swallow. All 35 liters (or 10 gallons) of it.

Like any binging, this will stop on its own, sooner than we realize - because we are not only binging

---

1   Compare to "Humanity's most lasting purpose has been to produce more humanity. Once that meant having as many children as possible, but the amount of kindness given to children has come to matter more than their number. Today humanity is above all an ideal of caring and kindness extending to every age and to every living being. The first rumblings of this historic shift were heard many centuries ago, but now large parts of the world are being shaken by it." Zeldin, Theodore, *An Intimate History of Humanity*, 1994, Sinclair-Stevenson, ISBN Hardcover 9781856194723 ISBN Paperback 9780060926915

2   Sieferle, Krausmann, Schandl, Winiwarter, 2006, *Das Ende der Fläche, Zum gesellschaftlichen Stoffwechsel der Industrialisierung*, Böhlau, Wien Köln Weimar, ISBN 978-3-412-31805-5 available, as far as I can tell, only in German

one day during the year, we are binging each and every single day. The hangover, I can assure you, will be epic!

In all this pondering, one particular data point has always fascinated me, one that both neatly and very scarily gets to the heart of the larger issue. In a highly developed agrarian society 1 Giga-Joule of labor together with photosynthesis generates from 4 to 7 GJ of food. 1 in vs. 4-7 out. In a fossil fueled society the equation is different. A given area of agricultural land uses in this society about 0.1 Giga-Joule of labor, 30 to 35 Giga-Joule of fossil fuels and photosynthesis to generate 25 to 35 Giga-Joule of food. 30-35 in vs. 25-30 out. On every single piece of agricultural land we put more energy in than we get out. Every day, everywhere, all the time. This is possible, because we use up the stored fuel it took millennia to create. And this is long before we consider the cost of erosion, of pesticides in run-off, of reduction in biodiversity, etc. Reduction in biodiversity, for example, is not just an unfortunate side effect of industrial agriculture, it whittles away at the resilience we rely on to protect us from calamity - day in and day out, until one day it'll snap.

To do this is bad enough, but to call it productive, efficient and fruitful - as we happily do in the economic frame - is either the height of stupidity or a conspiracy. If I were to ask you, where would you put your money? How would you answer my question? Leaning towards stupidity, or more towards conspiracy?

The Shortcomings of the economic narrative frame

The success of setting free the entrepreneurial spirit - another code for maximizing advantage - in a world of royal privileges and ever-present death from starvation must have seemed like magic to people at the time. OK, they got a very generous helping hand from the unlocking of fossil fuels, but still, the promise of a better future must have been electrifying. This is why new narratives frames take hold. Their promise of creating meaning for, of giving direction to and of putting structure into our daily lives in order to help us lead a life worth living is actually true. It is tautological: Unless this is true, they don't take hold. Because they take hold, it must have been true.

The idea that if you apply yourself diligently to a task, life would become better, if not for you, then for your children, was born with the economic frame. It created a *future* by giving time in the minds of everyday people a direction. Until then, time had been circular, with redemption, or damnation, occurring after death. The economic frame created a believable narrative around the promise of heaven on earth. Believable, because people saw it come true in their own lifetime. Today, we may bemoan the fact that our agriculture uses unbelievable inputs of fossil fuel to break even (energetically speaking), but the farmer saw and felt the 10-fold reduction in the input needed of his back-breaking labor.

The transition from a flat world to an exponentially rising one was by no means smooth and easy. You just have to read any book by Charles Dickens[1] or

---

1   https://en.wikipedia.org/wiki/Book:Charles_Dickens

The Jungle by Upton Sinclair[1] to get a feel of the pain and cruelty of these dramatic shifts. But for many, many years, and for ever more people, growth was good. The narrative succeeded brilliantly in giving sense to people's life. Over time, growth also turned out to be one of the better ways of resolving conflicts. Discrimination, unfairness and inequality could, and has been, covered up by *relative* improvements, even if the root causes where never addressed. A prime example of this are the social security systems throughout the world that are built, and only function, on the assumption of eternal growth.

So why is this section entitled *shortcomings*? Because, the frame no longer serves the sense-giving functions successful frames must. I used the analogy to cancer further up to suggest that there is such a thing as bad growth. At the end of its sense-giving run the economic narrative has had, education, public infrastructure, even public security has become organized solely according to the economic story. We have all become economic producers and consumers, each maximizing our own advantage, contributing to an ever-increasing nation's gross national product. We all try to buy at 2 and sell at 3, and when we are depressed, we go shopping – physically or virtually.

So yes, the economic story delivers more wealth, more cars, more text- and WhatsApp messages, more tourism, more movement, more dating opportunities, more web pages, more clicks, more likes, more of everything in fact. But it also delivers more

---

1 https://en.wikipedia.org/wiki/The_Jungle

burnouts[1], more substance abuse, more precarious jobs, more debts that people much younger than I will eventually have to pay off, more unemployment and underemployment especially amongst young people, more inequality and the question we ought to ask, does it, on balance, amount to a good life, to a life that we judge, when it's time to go, to have been well worth living?

If, in one of the richest countries on earth, namely my home country, large numbers of people after working all their lives only qualify for a retirement payment that is *below* the poverty line, then, I suggest, the answer is no.

I am not alone in this conclusion. I was surprised to read the other day that even the International Monetary Fund (IMF) - the keeper of the economic vision - entertains the idea, if ever so cautiously, that neoliberalism may have been oversold[2], albeit so far only by members of the IMF's *research* department. A much more brutal dismissal of the economic story is the book by Saskia Sassen: "Expulsions - Brutality and Complexity in the Global Economy", published by Harvard University Press in May 2014.

If you are more visually inclined, go see the movie System Error[3], as far as I know only in German.

1   This book is, as far as I know, only available in German. Still highly recommended: Martina Leibovici-Mühlberger, 2013, *Die Burnout-Lüge*, edition a, Wien, ISBN 978-3-99001-062-4. On page 184 the author writes: „Unsere heutige vorliegende Burnout-Gesellschaft ist der auf die Eskalationsspitze getriebene Konflikt zwischen dem Primat des zivilisatorisch begründeten ökonomischen Prinzips und unserer biologischen Natur. Und immer mehr von uns scheitern an der Verneinung des Menschlichen in uns – das nennt man dann Burnout."

2   Jonathan D. Ostry, Prakash Loungani, and Davide Furceri, 2016, *Neoliberalism: Oversold?* Finance & Development, June 2016, Vol. 53, No. 2, url: http://www.imf.org/external/pubs/ft/fandd/2016/06/ostry.htm accessed June 13, 2016

3   http://www.systemerror-film.de/

And then there is Tomáš Sedláček, who writes even more darkly that "the only thing remaining for us is growth – growth which knows nothing but itself, because it has no goal to measure. The feeling of aimlessness binds it to meaninglessness and homelessness"[1]. He goes on on the next page to say that "if maximum growth is the imperative of our time, at any cost, then true rest and satisfaction are not possible." Mr. Sedláček, I'd like to point out, is an eminent *economist* from the Czech Republic.

I believe it is this feeling of senselessness, this feeling of no longer being able to assemble all the damn things that happen one after another into a meaningful narrative with an internal logic, dynamic and rhythm that is the real reason we are coming up with the next large story for humanity. "[A] feeling of aimlessness [bound] to meaninglessness and homelessness", as Sedláček writes, fails miserably at giving you a reason to get up in the morning and try to make it through another day.[2]

> *Even if you win at the rat race,*
> *you're still a rat.*
> T. Bill

And yet, *why* is this so? The answer to this question led me to the field of happiness research where I

---

1 Tomáš Sedláček, 2013, Economics of Good and Evil: The Quest for Economic Meaning from Gilgamesh to Wall Street, Oxford University Press, pg. 241, ISBN 978-0199322183

2 There are other, more intellectual, arguments why the economic story has run its course. Two good ones, though lengthy and written in the jargon of sociology, are Wolfgang Streeck, 2014, *Buying Time: The Delayed Crisis of Democratic Capitalism*, Verso, London and New York, ISBN: 9781781685488 and Karl Polanyi, 2001 [1944], *The Great Transformation, The Political and Economic Origins of Our Time*, Beacon Press, Boston, USA, ISBN: 978-080705643-1 Polanyi speaks of the fact that life has become a mere adjunct of, subservient to, the motive of gain.

ran across the World Happiness Council[1] and their World Happiness Report. Good solid data also come from Esteban Ortiz-Ospina and Max Roser at Our World in Data[2]. Their graph of GDP[3] vs. Life Satisfaction in their section II.1 caught my eye (you should also make the effort to look it up, link is in the footnote 2 below). At first glance it confirms the promise of the economic frame: more is better. The line that your eye and brain instinctively draw is a straight line, gently but steadily rising from bottom left to top right. It is the iconic graph of the economic story, exemplifying beautifully what I wrote earlier about images and numbers in one memorable picture.

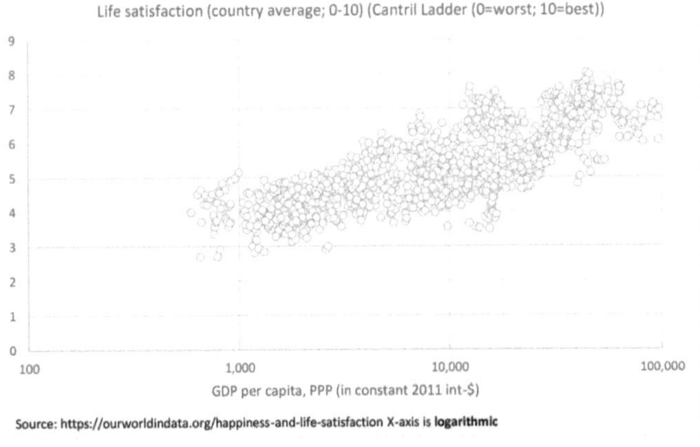

Source: https://ourworldindata.org/happiness-and-life-satisfaction X-axis is **logarithmic**

The graph shows 1420 data points of all countries in the world at various times between 1700 and 2016. The GDP data is given in constant international

1   http://www.happinesscouncil.org/
2   Esteban Ortiz-Ospina and Max Roser (2018) – "Happiness and Life Satisfaction". Published online at OurWorldInData.org. Retrieved from: ‚https://ourworldindata.org/happiness-and-life-satisfaction' [Online Resource]
3   https://www.quora.com/In-laymans-terms-what-does-gross-domestic-product-mean-GDP   and   https://simple.wikipedia.org/wiki/Gross_domestic_product

purchasing power parity (PPP) dollars – a fancy way of saying inflation and differences in purchasing power (a Big Mac costs more in Switzerland than in South Africa, even so it is the same thing) have been taken out – that is, you can compare the data across time and space.

The 'Cantril Ladder' (the vertical scale) is a measure of one's own life satisfaction. It asks respondents to think of a ladder, with the best possible life for them being a 10, and the worst possible life being a 0. They are then asked to rate their own current lives on that 0 to 10 scale.

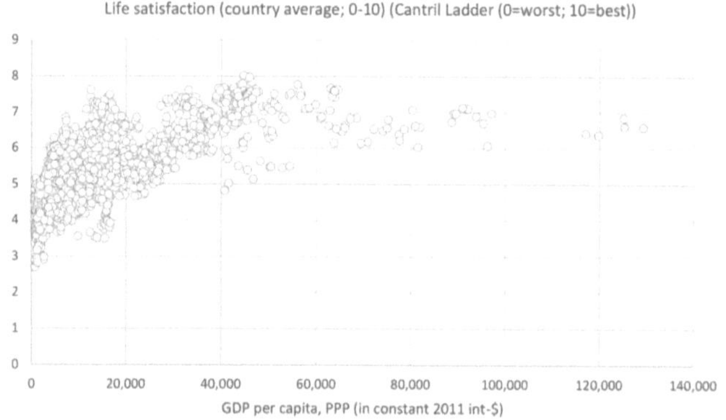

Source: https://ourworldindata.org/happiness-and-life-satisfaction X-axis linear, **not** logarithmic

It is only at a *second* glance that I noticed something odd: the x-axis, the one that runs horizontally at the bottom, has a logarithmic scale. Except for showing the strength of an earthquake (Richter scale) or the loudness of sound (decibel or dB), logarithmic scales are very uncommon and quite difficult to understand[1]. So, to make Ortiz-Ospina's and Roser's graph easier for me to understand I downloaded their data and plotted GDP per person on my x-axis

---

1   https://www.wikihow.com/Read-a-Logarithmic-Scale

and life happiness on my y-axis. On the opposite page is what I got.

Most of us are on the left, not surprising because, on average[1], the World GDP per person is around 10 000 dollars per year, in India around 5 000 dollars per year, in China around 13 000 dollars per year and in Africa below 5 000 dollars per year. Only Europe, at around 35 000 and the US at around 50 000 dollars per year and per person make it to the right of the graph. The dots beyond that are the truly rich, generally countries with very small populations like Singapore, United Arab Emirates and Luxembourg, for example.

Looking at the *non*-logarithmic graph, what is now your impression? Mine was that between 0 and 30 000 dollars per person per year (x-axis), where most of us live, there is an upward trend, meaning the richer you are, the more satisfied you are with your own life. But moving from 30 000 dollars per person per year even further to the right – where the really rich people live – very little happens on the life satisfaction scale. If you want to push it, yes, there may be a small increase, but if you compare the increase in life satisfaction you get from an increase in income from, say, 50 000 to 55 000 dollars per person per year it is really tiny compared with an increase in life satisfaction when income increases from 0 to 5 000 dollars per person per year.

The fancy way to say this is that there are diminishing returns (of life satisfaction) to increases in income: the richer you are, the smaller any further increase in life satisfaction becomes with even more

---

1   The average is a bad indicator for information about individuals, but for hundreds of data points from hundreds of years from across the world it is a good descriptor of humanity.

income. To make this effect more visible, I fitted a least square difference line over the data[1]. I got the graph below.

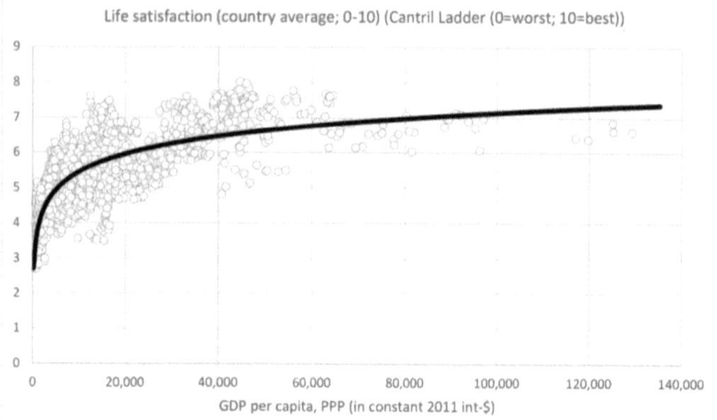

Source: https://ourworldindata.org/happiness-and-life-satisfaction X-axis linear, **not** logarithmic

That black curve answers the question of why the economic frame has reached the end of its line. The economic story is a sense-giving narrative frame at the bottom of Maslow's hierarchy of needs, when we are poor and mostly concerned with food, shelter and security. Way over on the left, when more material indeed means more life satisfaction. In money terms, this is the region between 0 and 10 000 dollars per person per year. In that region, there is a proportionality between income and life satisfaction. There the promise of the economic frame – more is better, and much more is much better – holds true because down there, we are all material-constrained.

Once we pass that threshold, we are no longer material-constrained, we are *meaning*-constrained. The world, on average, is at that tipping point. Increas-

1   'Fitting a line' is colloquial for finding the least square difference between the data and the fitted line. See https://en.wikipedia.org/wiki/Least_squares for more detail

ing our material well-being, as we did over the last 200 years will, in the future, no longer give us the life satisfaction we learned to expect from it. Yet, the economic story hangs on to our collective imagination with all its might. It is difficult to accept that what worked so well in the past no longer works in the present, nor the future. So, we, who have vivid memories of climbing up that curve, double our effort, increase our ruthlessness and work harder still – just as the economic frame urges us to do. But the curve above shows us that if you live at 30, 40, 50 and more thousand dollars per person per year getting to 60, 70, 80 and beyond won't make your life very much more meaningful. On the contrary, the "feeling of aimlessness [bound] to meaninglessness and homelessness" takes root – in your soul and in your heart, in your relationships and in your connections, in the world and in society. Life becomes wasted, empty and cynical.

And thus, we know it with all our senses that a new sense-giving narrative must emerge.

THE WORLD AS IT WILL BE: THE STORY OF GENEROUS RESPECT

> *"I don't want to lose my life by becoming one of the winners."*
> Anonymous

> *"For last year's words belong to last year's language. And next year's words await another voice."*
> — T.S. Eliot, *Four Quartets*

> *"If you want to build a ship, don't drum up the men to gather wood, divide the work, and give orders. Instead, teach them to yearn for the vast and endless sea."*
> — Antoine de Saint-Exupéry

The need to make sense of your life never goes away. But the narrative frames that help you do this, they come and go. Now that the economic frame is gone, what will take its place? To answer, I'll have to venture into the unknown. Because we will know for sure only afterwards. *After* the new frame has emerged, proven its worth and been recognized as such by everybody. But I am impatient and don't want to wait that long. Plus, the reason that old frames hang in there past their prime is not because they are still useful, they often hang on simply because nothing new has stepped forward to take their place. Like old politicians who can't let go. Actually, a bit like anybody who can't let go, once it's obvious to everyone but themselves that they should.

So, at the risk of writing something quite ridiculous, I will put forward my thoughts. Even if they do turn out to be besides the point, at least you will have learned from my attempt that one can and should do this. Maybe I'll inspire you to try yourself - and hopefully, your attempt will be better.

The promise of the next frame is to be taken seriously for who you are

If you recall Maslow's hierarchy, it starts with basic physiological needs (food, shelter, rest, security), moves up over belonging (intimate relations, friendships), esteem (prestige and feeling of accomplishment) all the way to self-actualization (achieving one's full potential, creativity). It is not that up on his pyramid the basic needs disappeared, but after 200 years of relentless material growth we can meet them with less than our full attention. We have time and are free to attend to these other – the social, psycho-social and self-fulfillment needs. Our great-grandparents needed to spend more than half of their income, time and attention on food, for example, we spend less than 5%, and often even less than 2-3% on the calories we need to survive[1]. Thus, we have time for the other needs.

You probably read quickly over the last sentence, hardly noticing its profound implications: **We have time** to attend to needs other than the basic physiological ones.

The economic frame is a wonderful sense-making frame when you need to spend all your time, all your effort, all your cunning to provide for the basic needs of food, warmth, rest and safety for yourself and your family. It fails to provide sense, guidance

---

1   Stanley Lebergott, 1995, Consumer Expenditures: New Measures and Old Motives, Princeton University Press

and direction to your life when you have time for social, psycho-social and self-fulfillment needs.

The deep irony is that it first needed the 200-year success story of the economic frame to lift us – on average – out of the abject poverty we all were in, in order to be able to attend to our social, psycho-social and self-fulfillment needs – where the economic frame as a giver of sense fails miserably.

These other needs, which cannot be met through material offerings, are as important for our well-being as the basic, material, ones. Once our basic ones are met, we *must* attend to the others. If we don't, our sense of life satisfaction suffers. But meeting them requires something different than material substitutes. If you are in need of love and attention, a diamond, no matter how valuable and no matter how sparkling, simply won't do. If you are in need of intimate friendship, likes, no matter how many, on the so-called social networks simply won't do. If your destiny is to be an artist or a healer, getting the 'employee-of-the-month' reward simply won't do.

To have your needs of belonging, of esteem and of self-actualization met you need deep, respectful and generous relations with others in the analog world. To accept them yourself and provide them to others, you need time and generosity.

Luckily, the economic frame, as a parting gift, has given us both. I already mentioned how easy it has become for ourselves to feed the hunger in our bellies, even though it has no answer to the hunger in our souls. Born to answer our *basic* needs, its answer to *every* need is: more and more and more stuff. Not realizing that needs beyond the basic ones do not require more material but time, attention and empathy. Since you have the time, you can be generous with it.

And the economic frame has also given us the ability to be generous in other ways. On the flat portion of the curve I showed a few pages back it does not matter to your life satisfaction if you are at 40, 50 80 or 100 thousand dollars per year. Thus, if you want to, you can go back to less income and in the process give away what you had – trust me, your life satisfaction won't suffer in the least.

The paradox is that the economic frame, by diligently growing our stock of material wealth over the last 200 years, has given us the tools – time and generosity – to feed the hunger in our souls. It is up to us to use this gift wisely, namely to take each other seriously for who we are. In all our splendor and all our faintheartedness, in all our humor and all our dullness, in all our energy and all our tiredness. We are more than economic man and woman, we are human and as Theodore Zeldin writes: "Today humanity is above all an ideal of caring and kindness extending to every age and to every living being. The first rumblings of this historic shift were heard many centuries ago, but now large parts of the world are being shaken by it."[1]

The ideal of the next frame will be respectful relations

New narrative frames always emerge, because they address a widely felt need. Ours, I submit, is to address our social, psycho-social and self-fulfillment needs. During its reign the economic frame

---

1   Zeldin, Theodore, *An Intimate History of Humanity*, 1994, Sinclair-Stevenson, ISBN Hardcover 9781856194723 ISBN Paperback 9780060926915

created, and then celebrated – through its focus on growth and maximizing advantage – a very strong emphasis on the individual. 'Very strong' has in its dying days almost become an *exclusive* emphasis. Forgetting that at its extreme, a collection of mere individuals, no matter how (self-)optimized, cannot survive, nor function. Ronaldo and Neymar alone did not win the soccer championship in Russia in 2018[1].

Cults of the individual are inevitably only possible on the fertile ground of a functioning community[2]. But schooled in the heroic frame, we pay attention to the individual, not the ground, nor its fertility. Forgetting that without the substrate, individuals are, at best, a lone voice in the desert. Still, "what is in it for me?" has become the rallying cry of the economic frame. The one we use instinctively to judge each and every transaction we enter, commercial, personal, social. Not surprisingly, this has resulted in a pervasive lack of respect for the other. If I care only about the benefit for me in the current transaction, I need not care about you – enough others are ready to engage in the next transaction, just think of Tinder and its look-alikes.

Without respect, though, it is impossible to meet your social, psycho-social and self-fulfillment needs you need to meet to maintain your life's satisfaction. So, let's lean back, close our eyes and imagine a different world, governed by respectful relations:

One where young people have a real chance of building a life without being passed on from one

---

1   See Bertolt Brecht, Fragen eines lesenden Arbeiters at, for example, http://ingeb.org/Lieder/werbaute.html
2   Putnam, R. D. (2000). Bowling alone: The collapse and revival of American community. New York: Simon & Schuster.

internship to the next, one with real pay and real opportunity to learn.

One where women all over the world are treated as equals in the workplace, also and especially when it comes to their paycheck.

One where labor costs of your 400 USD smartphone are more than 4 USD per unit.

One where we are free to take care of those in need.

One where we do not plunder nature for our short-term enjoyment.

One where not one in five young people are completely without a job, as is the case in the European Union[1]. Next time you ride a tram or bus, look at the young and make a mental count.

One where old people are not stored in old people's homes and treated like imbeciles.

One where young researchers can build their career, without an endless succession of short-term contracts.

One where migrants, old and young, are treated as humans and not automatically assumed to be freeloaders who should be returned to where they came from.

One where old people can get a job, because their experience and knowledge is valued.

One where sick people do not get the distinct feeling they only exist to generate revenue for the health care system each time they go to the doctor.

---

1   http://ec.europa.eu/eurostat/statistics-explained/index.php/Unemployment_statistics accessed April 18, 2016

One where low paid workers are not replaced at the drop of a hat.

One where the animals we eat for food are not raised by ruthlessly minimizing the cost so our advantage is maximized.[1]

One where all people are treated as humans and not as "human capital", rationalized away at the whim of their employer.

One where ill people get the medication they need without having to pay tens of thousands of dollars per dose.

One where 1% of the world population does not own 50% of the planet's wealth[2]. I couldn't comment better on this than Warren Buffet once did: "There's class warfare, all right," Mr. Buffett said, "but it's my class, the rich class, that's making war, and we're winning."[3]

One where you don't need to ask: "what's in it for me?" but can ask "how can I help you?"

Once you get to dreaming of a different world, the floodgates open. So, before you read on, really do close your eyes and let your hopes and imaginations flow awhile. And when you're ready to return to this world, make sure you have pencil and paper ready

---

1   https://en.wikipedia.org/wiki/Intensive_animal_farming accessed April 18, 2016. A most disturbing video hosted by Paul McCartney is here: https://www.youtube.com/watch?v=ql8xkSYvwJs you need to verify your age in order to be able to watch it.

2   https://www.credit-suisse.com/ch/de/about-us/research/research-institute/publications.html scroll down. Accessed April 18, 2016

3   Ben Stein, *In Class Warfare, Guess Which Class Is Winning*, New York Times, Nov 26, 2006, http://www.nytimes.com/2006/11/26/business/yourmoney/26every.html?_r=1& accessed April 18, 2016

to jot down the highlights of your dreams. We'll need them later on.

The common thread that connects all these dreams is respect and relations. If you respect, and relate to your young research assistant, you don't make them grovel for crumbs once a year. If you respect and relate to ill people, you build a health care system that puts them, their illness, their fears and worries at the centre. If you respect and relate to your employees, you do not think of them as cost factors. If you respect and relate to old people, you do not create a society where they are stored in special enclosures. If you respect and relate to nature, you do not use up energy that it took a *million* years to form in just a *single* year. If you respect and relate to your fellow citizens, you don't make them work all their lives with lousy pay, and no chance to build up their retirement fund. Just because you *can* do something doesn't mean you *should*.

Too bad they are dreams - so far. But nothing stops us from starting to build a world where these dreams become real. Remember, we *can* be generous, and we *do* have time. But before you draw up the blueprints for the new frame, you yourself need to get into the habit to yearn for the vast and endless sea - and then work on instilling this yearning in others. As Betty Sue Flowers never tires of repeating: "The present is determined by the stories you tell about the future." Let's all get the ball rolling by telling a story of a future of relations and whose ideal is respect.

To give you faith that though this task is daunting, it is perfectly doable, let me remind you of what Yuval Harari's writes about our ability to talk about things that do not exist: "These imagined realities exert *real* force in the *real* world." (Harari 2015, emphasis added)

The archetypical actors of the new frame will be mediators and intermediaries.

Today, you meet in one planeload of people on their way to sun, sand and sailing more cultures than your great-grandmother did in her lifetime. Well, if you could actually meet them rather than being squeezed into a seat that feels smaller than the average industrial chicken has available in its short and brutish life.

The point is that in our connected world, the people around you most likely won't be 'like you'. They'll have different histories, different outlooks, different habits and different views of the world and of life. While really deep down all people want only two things, namely to love and to be loved, in everyday encounters the intricate layers of our differences tend to stand out.

Evolution has taught us to meet 'the other' with skepticism, which seemingly inevitably leads to prejudice, assignment of guilt and eventually fear. Evolution is also slow, slower than molasses crawling up a hill. So, we can't sit back and wait for evolution to learn and then teach us that in a connected world of 7 billion people, we need to meet 'the other' with curiosity, compassion and courage. Because, in the meantime, things will blow up.

Luckily, evolution has also given us culture[1] and through the cognitive revolution - remember, this is our ability to create stories about things that don't (yet) exist - we are well-placed to help evolution out in this matter. We can speed things up - as we must.

Here is how. Each society has members that have more empathy than others, with antennas that are much more sensitive than the average. They are the ones who will take the lead in mediating the countless irritating differences so that something new and complete can emerge. Since we are at best at the beginning of this, it is hard to find the right words to talk about this - *and next year's words await another voice*, as TS Eliot puts it - but let me try with an analogy.

If you consider the cells in your body, they are, though all originating from only two initial cells, as different as any collection of folks on that plane I mentioned. Yet they cooperate to create you, your looks, your thoughts, your gait, your humor. Not too long ago, we thought that for this to happen, there had to be someone in charge, directing all this. And the most usual suspect was the brain. As we learn more and more about ourselves, that picture is being replaced by an understanding of intricate bottom-up self-learning, self-healing and self-organizing processes at many, many levels. Even involving 'strangers': it is said that there are more microbes in and on each one of us, especially in our gut, than there are stars in the universe. With-

---

1   There are many definitions of culture. One I like is „Culture: learned and shared human patterns or models for living; day- to-day living patterns. These patterns and models pervade all aspects of human social interaction. Culture is mankind's primary adaptive mechanism", from Damen, L. (1987). *Culture Learning: The Fifth Dimension on the Language Classroom*. Reading, MA: Addison-Wesley, pg. 367

out them, we'd be dead[1]. Information, energy and material is passed, blocked, amplified and bundled through many pathways, blood in its vessels, hormones, nerves, connective tissue, the lymphatic system, etc. all working together, constantly mediating in other words, to create the whole you call yourself. And tend to recognize when you see yourself in the mirror.

For the body, we have a language and concepts to get a handle on this mediating, this working together for a common good without denying the exquisite individuality of each cell. For larger units, like a family, a group, a society, nation or even humanity, we still lack it. Even though some heroic attempts have been made[2], but they never got real traction. So, this is one of first items on our to-do list for the new narrative frame: Invent the proper words and concepts for mediation and intermediaries, and their work, on a social level[3]. While you may think it is odd to embark on a new frame without everything thought out ahead of time, I would like to remind you that the theoretical underpinnings of the economic frame were also only developed over the frame's lifetime. The yearning, we learn, is always ahead of the blueprints.

Seen against the background of the economic frame with its merciless quest for growth that devours everything in its path, mediators as the archetypical actors of the new frame sounds quaint. But, it is the *background* that is odd, *not* the mediating. It has

1 You have to read this book: Giulia Enders, 2015, *Gut: The Inside Story of Our Body's Most Underrated Organ*, Greystone Books, ISBN 978-1771641494
2 The most heroic, to my mind, is this book: James G Miller, 1978, *Living Systems*, McGraw-Hill, New York, ISBN 0-07-042015-7
3 To get you started and inspired, read Malcom Gladwell, 2000, *The Tipping Point*, Little Brown & Company; ISBN: 0316316962 where he talks of mavens, connectors and salesmen.

deep roots in the religious frame: "Blessed are the peacemakers: for they shall be called the children of God." Even more importantly, it is the peacemakers who create the conditions for life[1], warriors only destroy.

A few paragraphs back, I said that each society has members more empathetic than the average and thus predestined to step forward as the 'pioneer' mediators and intermediaries. While pioneers are always needed to get something started, the good news is that we can all learn to be more empathetic – we'll be the 'follower' or 'hangers-on' mediators and intermediaries. Luckily, it is easy to learn empathy. How easy is illustrated by this little story. Malcolm Gladwell tells of an experiment[2] where a group of seminary students was split in two. One group was told to go to the next meeting across campus and as they were running late, they should hurry up. The other group was told to go to the same meeting across campus (by a different route) and they were told they had plenty of time. On their way, each group met a disabled person who needed help. And the really amazing, to me at least, result was that four fifth of those who were told they were running late did not help the disabled person, whereas four fifths of those who were told they had time, did stop and help[3].

---

1   https://www.newstatesman.com/politics/uk/2016/01/ending-new-thirty-years-war or https://afk-web.de/cms/ which is mostly in German and https://www.peacejusticestudies.org/index.php

2   Malcolm Gladwell, 2000, *The Tipping Point*, Little Brown & Company; ISBN: 0316316962, pg. 164

3   If you want to dig deeper into this phenomenon look for the research done on mirror neurons. A gentle way to start is https://en.wikipedia.org/wiki/Mirror_neuron and https://blogs.scientificamerican.com/guest-blog/whats-so-special-about-mirror-neurons/

So, relax, slow down[1], and your empathy will take wings. With it you can safely engage in respectful relations.

The language of the new frame will be feedback-stories.

Each frame, as we saw by looking at frames of the past, has an archetypical language. Recall that the economic frame's is images and numbers - *not* words. This matters tremendously. For good and for bad. For good: it allows the frame to be truly universal - good for the frame, not quite so good for us. For bad: all the nuances, all the subtleties, all the shades of gray that make up life in its full splendor are simply gone. Vanished. Poof.

The language of our next frame will reintroduce words in the form of stories. And add feedback models to the mix. Why?

Feedback

All structures and systems capable of surviving a certain amount of time – i.e. all living systems - are feedback systems, even more correctly, they are homeostatic feedback systems. And please note that homeostatic is NOT static! Homeostasis simply means the ability of a system to cushion, or to absorb variations in the world external to the system itself. For example, your body temperature is 37°C (or 98.6°F), plus or minus 1 to 2°C to feel well, plus or minus 4°C or so to be able to survive, despite it being outside a miserable -2°C on a gray and wet winter day, or 45°C in the desert. You, in other words, are a homeostatic system[2]. As is your

1   Respect is taking the time it takes.
2   Walter B Cannon, 1932, *The Wisdom of the Body*, Norton, New York, ISBN 978-0393002058

cat and your dog. Even more important, your family, your soccer team, your choir, your city and your nation are all homeostatic systems. They all withstand blows and adversity, they are resilient. That's what living systems do, day in and day out. They tirelessly bring you and your temperature, your blood sugar level, your gut flora, your hormones, etc. back into a balance. So you feel well.

Structurally, this is done by literally countless balancing feedback loops. A 'balancing feedback loop' has a goal, sensors to check if reality is in line with the goal and ways to set in motion action to bring reality closer to the goal - on and on and on. Meanwhile, reality has changed again, the sensors report the new deviation, the loop again sets in motion the appropriate action to bring reality once more closer to the goal[1],[2]. As long as you live. In fact, death could be defined as the breakdown, the cessation of the functioning of your balancing feedback loops.

You may wonder why these wonderful feedback loops don't just keep reality perfectly aligned to the goal, for good? Because in order to stay alive, you absolutely need these variations, the deviations of reality from its goal. A person whose vital signs show no variation any-more has "flatlined" – the next, and only, thing he or she needs is the service of an undertaker.

OK, one level deeper: why do you need these deviations? To learn: how you deal with deviations is largely a function of your coping skills. These skills are the strategies and actions you use, consciously

---

1 Ashby WR, 1960, *Design for a Brain: The Origin of Adaptive Behavior*, Wiley, New York, https://archive.org/details/designforbrainor00ashb
2 Pribram KH, 1971, *Languages of the Brain*, Prentice-Hall, Englewood Cliffs, NJ, USA, ISBN 0-13-522730-5

or not, to minimize the deviation between goal and reality[1]. To illustrate this, consider a person's food intake as an example. The goal reflects physiological need (calories, protein, fat, carbohydrate, minerals, and vitamins) modified by taste and availability. Actual food intake is the reality. Coping skills in this example range from an awareness of the need for food, the earning potential to buy it, and the skills to prepare it, all the way to the muscle coordination involved in lifting a fork and sipping a coffee.

These skills, in turn, need to be exercised to stay supple, to be ready to return you to your balanced condition. And how are they exercised? By dealing with deviations. It's the old 'use it or lose it' saying, and more properly, it is called learning.

If reality and goal are perfectly aligned over long stretches, your coping skills atrophy, they wither away and next time you'd need them, they are no longer available to you. One needs stress to build up coping skills, and coping skills are required to eliminate future stress. An old insight, first noted in 1968 by von Bertalanffy: Hence, "complete relaxation of tension as in sensory deprivation experiments is not an ideal state ... the psycho-social organism needs an amount of tension and activity for healthy existence."[2]

You can see this effect in old people. Their coping skills - say, to keep from falling - are diminishing as they get older. It is what we call the 'aging process'. So they tend to be very cautious to make sure they

---

1   On the physiological level the idea of coping skills is very well described by Hans Selye, 1956, *The Stress of Life*, McGraw-Hill, New York, ISBN 978-0070562127 and his book in 1974, *Stress without Distress*, Lippincott, New York, ISBN 978-0397010264

2   Bertalanffy L von, 1968, *General Systems Theory*, Braziller, New York, ISBN 978-0807604533, pg. 209-210

don't fall. Which reduces their ability to recover from a fall once it does happen. So they tend to become even more cautious - a downward spiral. The opposite can be observed with babies. Since they do fall and hurt themselves, nature equipped them with an ability to recover from falls that would fell an older person. Thus, babies lose their fear of falling and in the process build up their coping skills not to fall.

One could sum up the last several paragraphs in this equation: Life = deviation + feedback!

Feedback loops are thus the structural building blocks of everything that's alive. They are the expression of the adaptive capacity that is the essence of life. Thus, learning to use their terminology is not only neat, it's clever and parsimonious – because the difference between reality and your perception of it is not increased by using an inappropriate language. Meanings won't be lost in translation.

> *"Now that the silences produced by specialisation have become deafening, and now that information fills the air as never before, it is possible to reconsider the choice, to ask whether many people might not be better off if they began looking again for the road which leads beyond specialisation, if they tried seeing the universe as a whole".*
> *Th. Zeldin, An Intimate History of Humanity, pg. 198*

Feedback really matters when you have power

Now, those of you who paid close attention so far will chip in with the following comment: If, as you say, feedback loops are everywhere, how come we did not adapt our language to them in the past? How come, we got away with hero-stories, prayers, logic, math, images and numbers?

The reason is that until a few hundred years ago, anything we humans undertook did not matter on a geophysical, evolutionary scale. It mattered a lot to us individually, but the planet, nature and life itself just shrugged - if they noticed at all. (Left in the picture below)

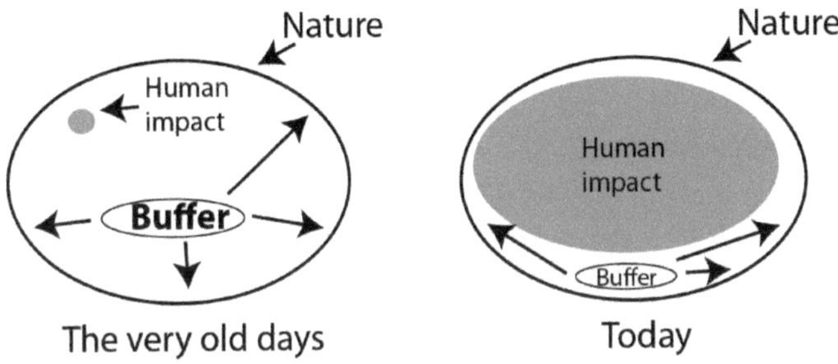

The very old days   Today

This has changed. Collectively, we now do matter. We change the climate, we leave behind waste that needs to be kept separate from life for tens of thousands of years, we intervene in evolution, to name but a few areas where learning by trial and error won't work any longer. Because the potential errors could wipe us out. (Right in the picture above)

In the past, before we mattered, our task was to adapt. While feedback loops have been busy in the background since the dawn of time, all we could do with our limitations was to adapt to very select portions of them. Now that we matter, we'd better understand them thoroughly, rather than casually, and knowing as best as we can, what the heck it is we're setting in motion, *before* we do anything. "Spitting in the wind get's back at you twice as hard", as Lou Reed already noticed in 1989.[1]

---

1   Lou Reed - *Strawman*, Lyrics © Sony/ATV Music Publishing LLC, SONY ATV MUSIC PUB LLC

With knowledge and power comes responsibility. While we have created elaborate ways to break that link – so that we can always pretend that *nothing* is really our fault – humanity as a whole needs to step up to the plate. The piper is impatiently waiting to be paid. Your contribution could be to become proficient in the language of feedback[1]. A side benefit of becoming skilled at seeing the world as balancing feedback loops is a deep calmness vis-à-vis the tribulations of everyday life. All those loops are busily and constantly at work, often quietly and in the background, to restore balance to your life. You are neither alone, nor do you have to carry the weight of the world on your shoulders all by yourself. How is that for a good night's sleep?

As you will realize when you begin to learn about feedback structures, they are the world's most powerful learning and understanding engines. They inevitably drive you to ask the right and the deep questions. But at the same time, they are the worst tool I can think of to communicate with. Hence, I now turn to their communicative cousins, scenarios.

Scenarios

Stories have two tasks. The first is to help us make sense of the world around us. As I mentioned at the very beginning, we humans are the story-telling

---

1   Since reframing the way we look at the world is social activity, let me start by recommending the book by David Peter Stroh, 2015, *Systems Thinking for Social Change*, Chelsea Green Publishing, White River Junction, VT, USA, ISBN 978-1-60358-580-4. If you want to go and study, start looking here http://www.systemdynamics.org/courses/ last accessed April 23, 2016 and here: http://simulation.tbm.tudelft.nl/smallSDmodels/Intro.html This is an e-Book and video course by Erik Pruyt

There has been for some time an attempt in the US to teach K-12 (kindergarden through 12th grade) students the language of feedback. See http://www.clexchange.org/ for more.

animal, capable of talking about things that do not exist. *We use stories to give meaning to events* that without them, would just be an endless procession of one damn thing after another. This is the use of stories we are familiar with. This is how we explain the world, its wonders and its injustices to our children when they grow up. This is how tribes and societies use myths about their creation to give meaning to who they are. Myths, used here in an ambiguous sense: once in the sense of an old story, told and retold throughout the ages[1]; and also in the sense of 'not necessarily true', since the task of a myth is to reaffirm in the present an idea of creation, not to be truthful to real events at the time of creation. That has been the task of stories so far: helping us to make sense by *explaining* with an inner logic and dynamic how the world around us works[2].

Hence, we are experts at story-*evaluation*. We can tell in a split-second if a story works, hangs together, makes sense - or if someone is trying to pull the wool over our eyes by telling a tall tale. "You can fool all the people some of the time, and some of the people all the time, but you cannot fool all the people all the time," as Abraham Lincoln is reputed to have said. Even your two-year old will call on you if she's unhappy with her bed-time story.

Recently, stories have taken on a *second* task. Mainly as a consequence of the geophysical power humans have gained. With so much power at our disposal that we can alter the climate, change evo-

---

1   For the best introduction on myths read Joseph Campbell, 1972, *Myths to live by*, Viking Press, New York, ISBN 978-0-14-019461-6

2   Though using different words, this explanatory task is what is done by what Daniel Kahneman calls 'System 1' in his book *Thinking, Fast and Slow*: Kahneman, D. (2011). Thinking, fast and slow. New York: Farrar, Straus and Giroux.

lution and wipe out all life on our planet, merely adapting isn't good enough anymore. We need to *pre*-think our possible actions and inactions as to their impact into the far future. Saying "what can I do, I am just a little multinational", as a CEO of a North American utility once told me in an interview, is grossly inadequate. Yet we hear – and say – it all the time, it's pitiful.

Since scenarios are stories of futures that could be, they are perfectly suited for this second, the *anticipatory*, task. This task, anticipating the consequences of our actions or inactions, is truly revolutionary, because our usual way of learning is by trial and error. Crudely put, the latter amounts to saying that even though I don't have the foggiest idea of what I am doing, I'll do it anyway, just to see what happens - who knows, something good may come of it. And if it doesn't, well I'll chalk it up to experience.

How deeply this way of approaching the future is in us can be seen by the proverbs we have created: 'If you are not willing to risk the unusual, you will have to settle for the ordinary.' 'Only those who will risk going too far can possibly find out how far one can go.' And, of course, the classic: Nothing ventured, nothing gained. Makes perfect sense only if, however far you *do* go, it doesn't mean anything to life on earth. At worst, you do terrible harm to yourself - but life on earth goes on. Not so smart, however, when your blindly charging ahead without thinking has the potential to do serious harm to lots and lots of others, across space and across time.

Well, guess what: we are in this latter stage. And not just because there are a few people in the world who, with the push of the nuclear button could wipe us all out. Even in less dramatic situations like the following: A premium breeding bull these days has tens of thousands of descendants, let's hope he is genetically fit. If viruses had sat down together a few decades ago to plan for their world-wide spread, at the very top of their list of strategic actions would have been the worldwide and constant movement of people - their gracious hosts - on planes criss-crossing the planet[1]. Feeding ever more people with a handful of industrially and mono-culturally grown and multiplied grains. Creating a global mono-culture through our smartphones[2] and thus wiping out the last pockets of resilient differences. Running all enterprises, whether commercial or not, along the lines of ferocious cost efficiency algorithms according to the latest profit-maximizing guru from the number one business school in the world. Feel free to add your own suggestions.

If we can't turn the clock back, if we can't put the lid back on Pandora's box - as I fully believe we cannot - then we should at least do the second-best thing, which is spend a little time thinking through *beforehand* what we set out to do. Since we've never really had to, the tools to do so are thin on the ground. One of the few I know that *everybody* can use, is to *create* scenarios. The 'everybody' is very important, because it's no use to outsource this task to others. We all have to become proficient in it, because we all have the power to influence life and the future. I know there are days when we don't feel we have that power, but simply by being alive in the 21st century, we do.

---

1   Did you know that at any moment in time there are about 700 000 people in planes moving to and fro? That's a rather large city on the move all the time.
2   I have to admit, a stroke of marketing genius to call this surveillance device a smart phone.

Thus, for the second task of scenarios, the anticipatory one, we must learn to *create* them. Not just tell and re-tell old stories. But to create them from scratch. There are some good books to help you do that[1]. Hopefully without sounding too arrogant, I recommend my book *Scenarios - How to create them and Why you should*[2]. It is a short, 100-page book, but still has everything in it you need to create your very own set of scenarios, by yourself or with your friends. You can get it for the price of two decent cups of coffee.

The behavior of the new frame will be empathetic service.

I need the word *empathetic* in order to distinguish the kind of service in the next narrative frame from the more common service we know from the economic story, where 'service' often has overtones of both hierarchy and submission. In the economic story, I serve you to get your money - end of story.

In the emerging frame the motivation of service is the desire to do what is in my power, so that *you* can better realize *your* full potential – so that *you* can better meet *your* social, psycho-social and self-fulfillment needs. This may be as basic as getting well after an illness, and it may be as esoteric as me trying to help you find meaning in your life. Perhaps the word esoteric is wrong here because isn't that what every parent should be guided by when they raise and educate their children? But in the economic story raising and educating a child is often

---

1 For example, Kees van der Heijden, 2004, *Scenarios: The Art of Strategic Conversation*, Wiley, Chichester, UK, ISBN 978-0-470-02368-6 and G. Wright and G. Cairns, 2011, *Scenario Thinking: Practical Approaches to the Future*, Palgrave Macmillan, London, New York and Shanghai, ISBN 978-0230271562

2 https://www.bod.de/buchshop/scenarios-ulrich-golueke-9783842344945

reduced to giving him or her a head start so that she or he can later on in life merely continue to maximize their advantage – the question of whether such a life leads to a contented life is rarely asked.

Empathetic service sounds odd at first. Why should I give you a head start? Won't you just use that advantage for your own ends? Against me? Note, though, that the worried conclusion – if I help you, won't you use this help I've given you against me – is only reached in the economic frame. In the new frame of generous respect, the conclusion is that the other one will do what is in her or his power to help *me*, in turn, to reach my potential. Biologists have a word for this, symbiosis. Psychologist and sociologist are still struggling to find one. Maybe, by the time you read this, they have some suggestions, as 'empathetic service' is a bit stilted. It also has the word 'pathetic' in it, which isn't good at all.

Once you start down this road of empathetic service you will notice that it comes around to you again. You will become part of a web of intricate relationships. This is not new to the human condition, it is, in fact, how we made us and our tribes more resilient to the vicissitudes of life and nature. For a good exposition of these ideas see Polanyi[1] pages 48 ff. where he writes that "[t]the outstanding discovery of recent historical and anthropological research is that man's economy, as a rule, is submerged to his social relationships." (It is well worth reading his next several pages.) It was only during the reign of the economic narrative that we tried, and failed, to cut the social relationships when they were in the

---

1 Karl Polanyi, 2001 [1944], *The Great Transformation, The Political and Economic Origins of Our Time*, Beacon Press, Boston, USA, ISBN: 978-080705643-1

way of maximizing our individual advantage. At last, we are, in the new frame, coming home.

By behaving with empathetic service, we are also getting closer to a truly ancient advice about what a life worth living might be. All major religions of the world stress that one way to heaven is by helping others. Written down during times of abject material poverty the examples they use are often material examples. Like St. Martin, who is said to have cut his coat in two to give one half to a naked beggar.

Marriage can also serve as a good illustration of respectful relations. For most of our history, marriage was, first and foremost, an economic affair. Arranged in one form or another, with strict rules about dowries, acceptable options after the death of one of the partners, marriage was meant to smooth out otherwise catastrophic impacts: floods, rotten harvests, locusts, disease, loss of jobs, marauding armies. Against such a background the purpose – also in a marriage – was to be obedient and to maximize advantage, concepts from the previous frames. Once the economic necessity of marriage is removed, we could – conceivably – marry for love and help the other to come ever closer to whatever their destiny may be. If you choose that path, all you can do is inspire your partner so that he or she may, in turn, choose to love you. And remember, in the new frame we *can* be generous, and we *do* have time.

The energy of the new frame will be solar - again.

You could say that all the energy we ever used, including the fossil one, is solar. Fossil fuels in that view are simply stored reserves - albeit over an incredibly long time, namely millions of years - of solar energy which we binged on over a few short hundreds of years. We are coming to the end of that binge, not necessarily because we have run out of fossil fuels, but because the planet and especially the climate portion of the planetary system is reaching its limits of accommodating the numerous waste products generated by their use. That, and the incredibly relative cheapness of renewables. Which becomes truly significant if you take into account really all incidental costs.

Speaking of 'incidental' costs, let me also remind you that nuclear power, sometimes touted as a renewable power because it emits no CO_2, never was able to even pay its own way. The risks of an accident were uninsurable from the start. Societies had to cap private liability, otherwise it would have been impossible to run any nuclear power plant at all. 'To cap' means to transfer the liability to the general public - a textbook example of privatizing the upside and socializing the downside. The pattern was set in the United States with the Price–Anderson Nuclear Industries Indemnity Act[1], first passed in 1957 and, in amended form, still valid today. Virtually all societies that use nuclear power have followed suit.

The solar energy of the new frame will be significantly different from the solar energy of the heroic, the religious and the scientific stories in the past, because our knowledge of how to use highly distributed, low density energy all coming ultimately from the sun is far advanced over what it was 300 years ago. We've learned how to store solar energy[2];

---

1 https://en.wikipedia.org/wiki/Price%E2%80%93Anderson_Nuclear_Industries_Indemnity_Act last accessed April 26, 2016
2 http://www.popularmechanics.com/science/energy/a9961/3-clever-new-ways-to-store-solar-energy-16407404/ last accessed April 27, 2016

we've learned how to increase the efficiency factor of all our machines[1]. We've begun to learn how to move from high temperature, high pressure and centralized chemistry to the low temperature, low pressure and decentralized kind, and we've learned to fly around the world on a solar powered plane[2]. I invite you to add to the list of examples where solar energy in the 21st century is not like solar energy in the 18th.

Using solar energy is also a sign of respect. You are not leaving a gigantic and toxic mess behind for endless future generations to take care of.

Visually, the summary of the new frame in my matrix look like this:

---

1   Carey W. King, John P. Maxwell and Alyssa Donovan, 2015, *Comparing World Economic and Net Energy Metrics, Part 1: Single Technology and Commodity Perspective*, Energies 2015, 8(11), 12949-12974; doi:10.3390/en81112346 esp. Fig 9 last accessed April 27, 2016
2   http://www.solarimpulse.com/ last accessed April 27, 2016

	Hero	Religion	Science	Economy	Generous respect
Promise	Survival	A good life after death	A good life here on earth	Material wealth for all, now	Being taken serious for who you are
Ideal	Excellence	Goodness	Truth	Growth	Respectful relations
Actors	Heroes Adversaries	Saints Prophets	Philosophers Scientists	Consumers Business	Mediators Intermediaries
Language	Stories	Scriptures Prayers	Logic Mathematics	Numbers Images	Feedback Stories
Behavior	Competition	Obedience	Reason	Maximizing Advantage	Empathetic service
Energy	Solar	Solar	Solar	Fossil	Solar

HOW TO GET THERE FROM HERE

I am neither the first to bemoan the emptiness and senselessness of the economic narrative frame, nor to dream of a better future. A future where the economy is once more an adjunct to humanity, rather than the other way around. The difficulty is always how to get there from here. Usually, at this point you can hear the talk of 'path-dependency'[1], on 'the true nature of human beings' - which is supposedly egoistic, hedonistic, self-centered and extremely short-sighted, on 'the economic frame, while being not ideal, still being the closest thing to perfection we have' and on countless other explanations that serve to convince you that the way things are is unchallengeable. A Mainer would more honestly say: You simply cain't get there from here.

But is true? Not really: We have had different narrative frames in the past to help us make sense of our lives, so why wouldn't it be possible to have different ones in the future?

Narrative frames, as I mentioned in the beginning, have a task to do, they don't just hang around for nothing. They need to help us humans give meaning, direction and structure to our lives, and by doing so, help answer the question of what is a life worth living. That task is always situational, a fancy way of saying that the solution must be relevant to what is going on in the lives of those who seek meaning, who want to get away from that one-damn-thing-after-another routine. Situations change, from the

---

1   A somewhat tongue-in-cheek explanation and example of path dependence is Dave Praeger, 2007, *Our Love Of Sewers: A Lesson in Path Dependence,* Daily Kos, http://www.dailykos.com/story/2007/06/15/346883/-Our-Love-Of-Sewers-A-Lesson-in-Path-Dependence last accessed April 26, 2016

hunting & gathering way of life, via agricultural and industrial societies to our post-modern society with its gross inequalities, its emptiness and senseless-ness. A one-size-fits-all frame is not up to the task. As situations change, so do frames.

How much effort is needed – to help bring forth the new generous frame?

> *"All empires become arrogant. It is their nature."*
> — *Edward Rutherfurd, New York*

Surprisingly little. If you think of dominant frames as empires of the mind, you'll be on the right track. While they reign supreme – empires and dominant frames alike, they are mighty, intimidating and invincible. Actually, *seemingly* invincible. Because within their strength are already the seeds of their demise. These seeds, inevitably, are 1) the tendency to spend more and more resources on the survival of the empire, or dominant frame, itself, rather than on serving the constituents for whom the empire was created; 2) empires and frames over-reach themselves; and 3) the tendency to shut themselves off from (critical) feedback, i.e. they stop learning.

You recognize the first seed of the demise in the eco-nomic frame's ever more blatant way that the frame serves its own elite, who, in this frame, are the rich. I already cited Warren Buffet above, you can look up the World Inequality Report[1], you can note how raising taxes has become taboo in just every coun-try you can think of and you can study the last tax reform in the US[2].

---

1   https://wir2018.wid.world/
2   https://www.bloomberg.com/view/articles/2018-05-04/
     trump-s-tax-cuts-still-don-t-seem-to-be-helping-u-s-workers

You recognize the second seed of demise in the way that every last corner of life is being subjected to the economic frame's ideal of growth and maximizing advantage. Not just what we think of as traditional commerce but areas like health care, prisons, old age care, education, from kindergarten all the way to universities, politics, art, leisure, dating, dying, you name it[1]. As one CEO in an interview once told me: "Sustainability is the last chance for humanity – but I am not sure we can afford it."

And the third seed of demise you recognize by the fact that all positions of power are held by, or advised by, main stream economists[2,3,4]. There are economists who question the orthodoxy of the economic story, but they are peripheral to it[5]. The center tolerates no dissent.

Thus, the economic frame is more of a 'Schein-riese', an *illusionary* giant, than a real one. More like

---

1   Mark Skousen, 2002, The Power of Economic Thinking, Bna Books, ISBN: 978-1572462014
2   https://www.theguardian.com/commentisfree/2013/oct/28/mainstream-economics-denial-world-changed
3   Fingleton, E. (2003). Unsustainable: How economic dogma is destroying American prosperity. New York: [s.l.]: Thunder's Mouth Press, Nation Books; Distributed by Publishers Group West.
4   ‚Economics has become the organising principle, the reigning ideology, and even the new religion of our time. And this body of knowledge is controlled by a selective priesthood trained in a very particular type of economics - that is, Neoclassical economics. In this penetrating analysis, based on very sophisticated theoretical reflections and highly original empirical work, the authors show how the rule by this priesthood and its disciples is strangling our economies and societies and how we can change this situation. It is a damning indictment for the economics profession that it has taken young people barely out of university to provide this analysis. Utterly compelling and sobering.' Ha-Joon Chang, Reader in Political Economy of Development at the University of Cambridge in a review of Joe Earle, Cahal Moran and Zach Ward-Perkins, 2016, The econocracy: The perils of leaving economics to the experts, Manchester University Press, ISBN: 978-1-5261-1013-8
5   https://en.wikipedia.org/wiki/Heterodox_economics

the wizard in the Wizard of Oz[1], who was unmasked by Toto, Dorothy's dog, by simply pulling a curtain and revealing a flabby middle-aged man. Illusionary giants are brought down by the mere push of someone's, often a child's, fingertip[2]. Because their previous power crumbles from within.

Before you push, though, it helps to prepare for the new frame. If the old frame crumbles without even a hint of something new, mayhem, turmoil and chaos is likely to emerge – and last for some time. Since the voices of experts, specialists and the powerful have fallen silent on what the new will be and who will bring it forth, it is up to us, you and me, to do this. What follows are some thoughts on what we can do to prepare.

Practical tips for the journey

Visit the future – starting with short excursions: How do things change? Immersed in the economic frame, where we all try to maximize our own advantage, all the time, we concluded that life is confrontational. Change, in the confrontational view, can only occur as a heroic clash between opposing viewpoints. That view makes for good, dramatic stories, but does not reflect what really happens. Change happens when you consistently, patiently and persistently do something - where each individual step by itself is often quite insignificant. Think of losing weight. Think of learning a foreign language. Think of learning to program an app. Think of cells dividing that lead to an embryo and then a human being. Think of falling in love. Think of nuclear fission that turns small amounts of matter into pure energy. Think

1   https://en.wikipedia.org/wiki/The_Wizard_of_Oz_(1939_film)
2   http://andersen.sdu.dk/vaerk/register/info_e.html?vid=17

of a marriage falling apart, of how trust is built and of how a tree grows.

So, the first bit of crucial advice is to actually *take* the first step. Which means being respectful to others and demand respect for yourself. Being generous to others and accepting their generosity in turn. Not, I hasten to add, in an ideological manner - but in a playful, fleeting manner.

Playful? Goes back to a saying of my late first mother in law: "You'll catch more flies with honey than with vinegar". Don't start out on your road into the generous and respectful frame by loudly and forcefully insisting that the other one first needs to acknowledge his or her disrespectfulness and do public penance, before you deign to bless them with your interest. If you only talk to saints, it'll be very quiet around you. Instead, take the first step and extend your respect and generosity to the other.

Fleeting? This is pragmatic advice to husband your strength. Coming from a frame that has excessively celebrated the individual above all else, you may find that the ability, the memory of how to treat others with respect and generosity has withered. Build up your strength as you go.

Practically speaking, start by designating a few hours in the week where you live the new paradigm. See how it feels, and if it feels right, extends the hours.

Visit the future together with others: On your excursions, and over time more generally, surround yourself with like-minded people. There are seven billion human people on this earth of whom you will meet a few hundred in your lifetime, and even fewer get to know really well – choose wisely! Together, it is much, much easier to change the world since we are not just the story-telling animal, we are also the social animal[1].

Be generous: Even those of us who have little can be generous with our time, with our attention, with our curiosity, with our empathy.

Islands of newness: In the middle ages, which we, with hindsight, often call the dark ages, monasteries with their libraries took on the role of preserving ancient knowledge[2]. Help create workshops, lectures, massively open online courses, associations, even communities that develop the ideas and ideals of the new frame further.

Learn the language: I mentioned above that the archetypical language of the new frame will be feedback-stories. Become proficient in understanding feedback loops and creating scenario-stories.

Recall your dreams: Remember when I asked you to note down your own dreams for the new frame? Now is the time to find that list, even add to it.

Bring the new frame into your current life: In your normal, economic-frame-life, inject elements

---

1 "Man is by nature a social animal; an individual who is unsocial naturally and not accidentally is either beneath our notice or more than human. Society is something that precedes the individual. Anyone who either cannot lead the common life or is so self-sufficient as not to need to, and therefore does not partake of society, is either a beast or a god." — Aristotle, Politics

2 Read Umberto Eco's *The Name of the Rose* to get a feel for that time. A more scholarly article on the 'Keepers of Knowledge' is Melissa Snell, How Knowledge and Learning Survived in the Middle Ages, available here: https://www.thoughtco.com/the-keepers-of-knowledge-1783761

of the new frame. Be generous without reason, respect others as a matter of course.

Know your limits: It is tempting to be a hero, but the dawning of the new frame does not rest on your shoulders alone. Always keep in mind the power and influence you have actually have and calibrate what you do accordingly. In between, take time to rest.

Don't give up: The major ingredient of change is persistence. Already the water drops that hollows the stone knows this. Or, as the English-speaking put it: 'Little strokes fell big oats.'

> *I'll get up and do it again*
> *Jackson Browne, The Pretender*

Gaming as learning: So far for humanity, the vast bulk of learning boiled down to matching an answer with a question. Finding an answer in the first place was left to the minor and major geniuses. And once one of those smart ones found an answer, the rest of us just needed to repeat it. In the new frame, largely freed from material constraints, learning becomes more like finding entirely new answers, and sometimes even entirely new questions. For this we need inductive, playful and pattern recognition skills, not rote learning. And those are the skills of Homo Ludens[1], not Homo Faber[2]. Again, the task will be easier than it looks at first: we all have used – usually very successfully – this method of learning in the first few years of our lives. It is only when we enter formal schooling all the way

---

1   Huizinga, J. (1955). *Homo ludens: A study of the play-element in culture* (First Beacon paperback edition.). Boston: Beacon Press.

2   https://roughghosts.com/2016/03/15/the-unmaking-of-man-the-maker-homo-faber-by-max-frisch/

to those executive retreats that we let those skills atrophy.

Play is more than simply releasing intellectual reserves that are buried deep inside every one of us. Games are known in every culture as safe spaces to test and develop new organizing frames. 'It is only a game' is one of the few spaces we have left to be able to look like a fool – without consequences. Which is why business games in corporations often do not work: everybody knows it is not really a game and you are being watched very, very carefully.

Use humor: It will be tricky for a while, since most humor is confrontational in our world. How could it be otherwise? The economic frame is about winning and losing, and if the law restricts me from hitting you on the head, at least I can make you look like a fool. Try to pay attention sometime to how much of our humor – also in advertising – is at the expense of someone else. A good way to start to change this is to make fun at yourself (this also avoids most, if not all, of the cross-cultural faux-pas that you never even know you are committing). Laughing at you yourself will also do wonders for your relations.

Develop your own moral compass: At the very edges or our existence, I believe, there is a right and a wrong, a truth and a falsehood, a black and a white, but most of our lives take place in the gray in between. The answers on how to behave in these gray zones have, in the past, been given by the need focus on material growth. That simplicity is over. In a meaning-constrained world we need to find, use and hone our very own moral compass. Sounds harder than it is. When we do something we should not do, we generally know, but often, far too often we do not listen – believe me, I know the feeling. Start to listen. Do not try to go from sinner to saint in one big step, pick three things you will do more of, three you will do less of and three you feel pretty right about. Do it alone and or with others, as is your habit. Watch yourself, revise, add to and delete from the list.

If you are lost and do not know where to start, have a look at the basic texts of any of the great religions. Antoine Saint Exupéry in his book "Flight to Arras"[1] once wrote that he only existed in the web of relationships that connected him with others. You weave and strengthen that web by being generous and showing respect. Only a few of us will wish to compete with Mother Teresa, but all of us can ask, how does my action, my words and my emotions help this other person in his or her quest to create meaning in their life.

Practice dilemmas: As we spend more time in the emerging meaning-constrained frame, dilemmas will arise that cannot be resolved objectively with a scientific experiment, or a statement from the Pope or the Supreme Court. Spend time with these dilemmas long before they become matters of life and death. Then you are ready when they do. Discover, nurture and reveal your ability to walk in someone else's shoes – for a while. Find out how 'negotiable' your identity really is. Where are your thresholds of discomfort, pain and with-drawal? In a world of no 'away' anymore, to agree to disagree is, at best, a temporary solution.

---

1   Antoine de Saint-Exupéry, 1969, Flight to Arras, Harcourt Brace, ISBN: 978-0156318808

Practice to go deeper, to a concept or an arrangement that shifts the focus from confrontation to creativity and healing – together. And do not forget to start with easy dilemmas.

Adjust your language: Beware of ways that language is changing to dehumanize humans. We have seen it before[1] and are seeing it again[2]. Use generous and respectful language.

Shift to your heart: The mind has had a good run for the last few hundred years. This makes sense, because the mind is simply very good when we had to remove material constraints. But, we have removed the material constraints. Now we embark on a road to tackle the meaning constraints. On this playing field the mind will play a subsidiary role; critical, yes, but subsidiary to the heart, the emotions, your generosity and respect.

Shift the question: While the fundamental question of the economic frame is "What is in it for me?" the guiding question of the new frame is "How can I help you?" Get used to using it.

Use the new frame in your profession: If you are a city planner, or a doctor, or a lightshow manager, or shelf-stacker in your local supermarket, or a refugee in a new country, or an investment banker, or a farmer, or a park ranger, or a nurse, or a professor, or an influencer, or a film-maker, or an economist, or a bus driver, or, or, or … try

---

1 https://en.wikipedia.org/wiki/LTI_%E2%80%93_Lingua_Tertii_Imperii, the book is here: Klemperer, V., & Brady, M. (2002). *The language of the Third Reich: LTI, lingua tertii imperii: a philologist's notebook*. London; New York: Continuum and https://en.wikipedia.org/wiki/Newspeak with the book here: Orwell, G., & Crick, B. R. (1984). *Nineteen eighty-four*. Oxford: New York: Clarendon Press; Oxford University Press.

2 https://www.vox.com/science-and-health/2018/5/17/17364562/trump-animals-dehumanization-psychology

to apply the guidance the new frame gives you in your daily professional life. Again, as I suggested at the beginning of this section, a little at first, an hour or so per week and then take it, slowly, from there.

And when you are ready, lift your fingertip and push.

When it's time, it's time.
Maine saying

YES – BUT ... WHAT ABOUT WORK?

Will there be commerce?

When I talk to people about the new generous and respectful frame most like it, to most it seems a refreshing change from the current one. But, sooner or later, they begin to wonder: "Will people still buy and sell things, will they have jobs, and will they get paid for the work they do?" The short answer is 'yes of course', the longer one goes like this: Just because the economic story will no longer be the dominant organizing principle, this does not mean that commerce will disappear. But it will be an adjunct to life, not its determining feature.

We live in a world where things have value because of effort. Effort involved in scraping the gold and other 'rare earths' from the mine, effort involved in going to school and work, effort involved in winning at sports, effort involved in raising a child. How much the effort in any one of the cases is worth is the realm of endless disagreements, conflicts and actual fights. Some call it the protestant ethic[1], some just call it the natural order of things – I would call it obvious, in a material-constrained world. To remove the material constraints requires effort and since this is what we needed to do (in a material-constrained world at the bottom of Maslow's hierarchy of needs) we value that effort.

This view of things is so ingrained in us that when we exert no effort, we are called lazy, do-nothings, free-loaders, forgetting that the automatic association of effort to value is, in fact, situational. It only makes sense in a material-constrained world. As we are leaving this one behind us to enter into a mean-

1   https://www.britannica.com/topic/Protestant-ethic

ing-constrained world, we need to rethink. Slowly, deliberately and thoroughly[1]. And I suggest we come to the conclusion that in a meaning-constrained world value is primarily created by trust.

Modern monetary theorists[2] are already there: They believe that money (value) is created by a bank making an entry in the creditors account. Why would banks do that? Because they trust the creditor to do something sensible with the money. If the creditor is required to lodge a security, then this means two things: 1) The bank does not trust the creditor quite so much and 2) the bank trusts the security more than the creditor. In all cases, it is a judgement of trust, nothing else. The element of trust has always been central to value creation. What changed is what we put our trust in: In the past we trusted that material stuff would be created, in the new frame we trust that meaning will be created.

Feels funny, doesn't it? But even in parts of the current economic frame we are already acting this way: for example, when it comes to valuing artistic 'effort'. If we paid Picasso only for the paint, brushes, canvas and his hours worked, his paintings would be a lot cheaper.

To put your worried mind even more at ease, think back to the transition from agriculture to the economic frame. The incredible folks at 'Our world in data' gathered data of the share of labor in agriculture from 1300 onwards for a handful of countries, shown on the opposite page.

---

1   This is to me a wonderful illustration of Kahneman's System 1 and System 2 way of thinking
2   https://en.wikipedia.org/wiki/Modern_Monetary_Theory

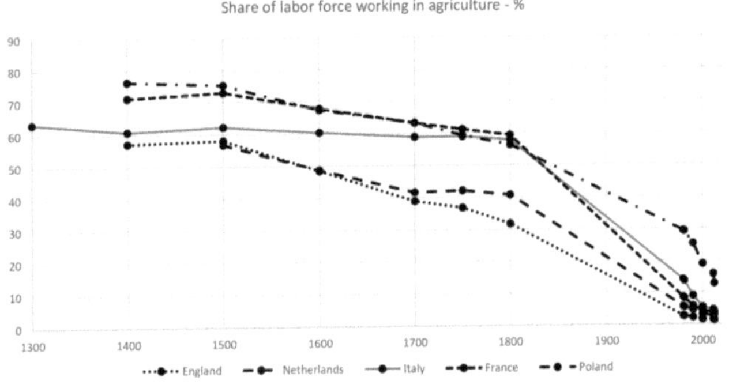

Source: https://ourworldindata.org/employment-in-agriculture

Before the economic frame unfolded its power, more than half of our forebearers worked in agriculture. 'Value' in that world was created by clearing the land, planting the seeds, picking the weeds, harvesting the grain, threshing the harvest, storing it safely, plus keeping the marauding soldiers at bay. Value was not created by digging the coal, drilling for oil, casting the metal, flying a plane nor programming an app. That all came later. The dramatic shift of employment between what we now call the three sectors of the economy can be seen if we pick one country as an example (see below).

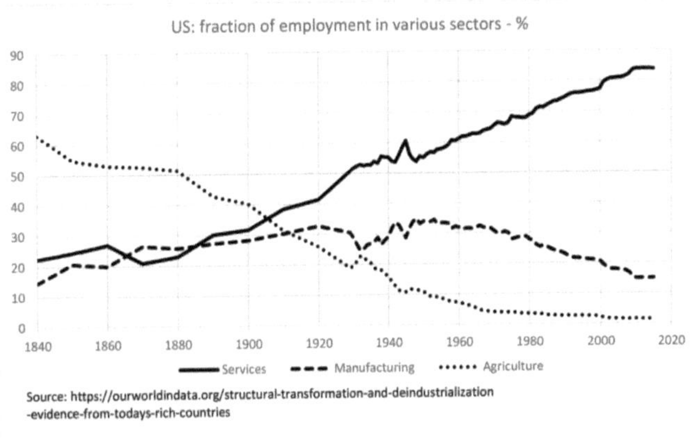

Source: https://ourworldindata.org/structural-transformation-and-deindustrialization
-evidence-from-todays-rich-countries

Over 80% - more than 4 out of 5 people – now work in services. If you'd be able to talk to my grand-father, who was a blacksmith and then changed to be an electrician, he wouldn't understand the world anymore. Like us, who are equally puzzled when it comes to understanding a generous and respectful world where material-constraints no longer rule our lives, something *we* can imagine because of the work our grand-fathers and grand-mothers did in their time.

What work will we do?

We are used by now to divide the economy into three sectors: agriculture, manufacturing and services. In the future, we will sub-divide services into those than can be done by machines (remember Moshe Vardi, whose quote started this book?) and those that cannot. The latter will be care, culture, creativity[1] and fulfilling social needs. Thus, the black solid curve in the last graph will bend downwards and a new, forth one will rise from meek beginnings to become the dominant one in the next story of humanity. Most of us will be busy in this forth sector to help each other – remember we are the social, story-telling animal – to meet our social, psycho-social and self-fulfillment needs. That will then be for us a life worth living.

What about disrespectful and ungenerous people?

There will be people in the new frame that are disrespectful, unkind, and not generous – including you who reads this and me who wrote this. None of us is

---

1   "An administration, like a machine, does not create. It carries on." Antoine de Saint-Exupéry, *Flight to Arras*

a saint. There are three ways to deal with them and with the sinner within each one of us:

Choose wisely. I had mentioned earlier the seven billion people on this earth, learn to recognize the ones who are generous and respectful, even just a little bit. Become friends with them; spend time with them; work for them; hire them.

Build up your strength. If you rest within yourself, if you are centered and if you are at peace with yourself it is much easier to tolerate the occasional contemptible person or action.

Confront them. If you are really brave, call them on their ungenerous and disrespectful behavior – in private. And if you are really, really brave, then in public. And don't forget to confront your own behavior when necessary[1].

Nothing is perfect, sighed the fox.
The Little Prince
by Antoine de Saint-Exupéry

---

1 Why do you look at the splinter in your brother's eye but don't notice the beam of wood in your own eye?

NOTES

"Humanity's most lasting purpose has been to produce more humanity. Once that meant having as many children as possible, but the amount of kindness given to children has come to matter more than their number. Today humanity is above all an ideal of caring and kindness extending to every age and to every living being. The first rumblings of this historic shift were heard many centuries ago, but now large parts of the world are being shaken by it."
Theodore Zeldin, An Intimate History of Humanity

"Don't blindly believe what I say. Don't believe me because others convince you of my words. Don't believe anything you see, read, or hear from others, whether of authority, religious teachers or texts. Don't rely on logic alone, nor speculation. Don't infer or be deceived by appearances. Do not give up your authority and follow blindly the will of others. This way will lead to only delusion. Find out for yourself what is truth, what is real."

Kalama Sutta: To the Kalamas[1]

---

1   https://www.accesstoinsight.org/tipitaka/an/an03/an03.065.than.html

Do you want to be right, or do you want to change the world?

WHO ARE YOU?

WHAT IS YOUR TASK?

WHAT DO YOU REALLY NEED?

WHEN THE STUDENT IS READY, THE TEACHER APPEARS. WHAT CAN YOU TEACH OTHERS?

UNCERTAINTY **IS THE CREATIVE GAP IN THE PRESENT THROUGH WHICH WE CAN INFLUENCE THE FUTURE.**

How much mercy can you show?